ABOUT THE AUTHORS

Brian Doyle FCA is founding Director and Executive Chairman of The Mentor Programme Ltd. He was responsible for the introduction and development of the Enterprise Ireland Mentor Programme and served as its Chief Executive.

He is a Chartered Accountant and has wide experience of the business world, having been Chief Accountant of the Irish Dairy Board, Managing Director of The Royal Trust Bank (Ireland) Ltd. and Group General Manager of Masstock Saudia. He is a Director of a number of Irish private companies. He can be contacted at brdoyle@iol.ie.

N. Vincent O Neill MA BComm FCA MInstM is Managing Director of Financial Controllers Ireland Ltd. He is also Director of a number of private companies in the data conversion, database management, building supplies and consumer products industries.

He has lectured extensively on management topics in Bahrain, Britain, Holland, Ireland and the USA. He has mentored over 100 enterprises, including manufacturing and service businesses, artistic societies and charitable institutions. He can be contacted at fci@eircom.net.

MENTORING
ENTREPRENEURS

Shared Wisdom from Experience

Brian Doyle and N. Vincent O Neill

Oak Tree Press
19 Rutland Street,
Cork.
http://www.oaktreepress.com
http://www.mentoringentrepreneurs.com

A catalogue record of this book is
available from the British Library.

ISBN 1 86076 230 1

Printed in Great Britain by MPG Books Ltd.

CONTENTS

ACKNOWLEDGEMENTS

We are pleased to thank the following for their helpful comments on various drafts of the book:

- John Doran and Mary Halpin of The Mentor Network, Enterprise Ireland, for their detailed comments on **Chapter 7**

- Gerry Wynne of Enterprise Ireland, who should have been a mentor, for his general advice on mentoring

- Bernard Dempsey, of the Mentor Network in Enterprise Ireland, for his help in finalising the assignment assessment questionnaire

- James Boylan for reading an early draft of three chapters and advancing advice which was taken

- Gerry Fitzmaurice, managing editor of the *North County Leader* newspaper, an experienced mentoree, for his views on the characteristics of an ideal mentor

- Raymond J. O'Kelly, managing director of the Data-conversion Group, who gave much time to reading drafts and making trenchant comments on clarity and relevance

- Professor John Dillon who traced the Abbé Fénelon for us

- Professor Kerill O Neill for sourcing material for **Chapter 11**

- Paul Targett for bringing to our attention the book, *Selling the Wheel*

- The late and sorely missed Professor Des Hally for his advice on training

- Osgar O Neill for reading chapters without protest

- And, although mentioned last, not the least, Catherine O Neill and Kay Doyle for their patient understanding and endurance of our literary efforts.

FOREWORD

I am very proud to have been the first Chairman of the Mentor Programme and to have been in at the beginning of an initiative that has proved so beneficial to Irish small and medium-sized enterprises.

It has been exciting to work with Brian and his colleagues on a professional approach to this very ancient concept. The administrative team and the panel of mentors brought together a wide variety of skills and expertise and formed them into a very powerful force to help in the development of small business in Ireland. The mentors recruited to the panel have brought not only their skills and expertise but also a sense of humour. They clearly enjoy the work they are doing.

This book would have been of enormous assistance to us had it existed back in 1988 when our initiative was first introduced. I know that its existence now will help potential developers of similar initiatives in the years ahead.

It is a book that should find a prominent place in the libraries of those charged with developing the potential of small business everywhere.

Dr Joseph C. McGough
First Chairman of the Mentor Programme

Enterprise Ireland firmly believes in the effectiveness of mentoring and we are delighted to have been involved from the beginning with the development of the concept of a co-ordinated and professional approach to mentoring of small business in Ireland.

The work done by Brian and all the panel of mentors, under the very capable chairmanship of Dr Joseph C. McGough, has made a significant contribution to the success of Irish small business and we are confident that its influence will continue long into the future.

In the early pioneering days of the programme, there were many aspects that were explored on a trial and error basis. Some worked, some didn't. If this book had existed then, we would have been saved a considerable amount of time and the frustration of sometimes going down blind alleys.

Enterprise Ireland is delighted to be a sponsor of this book and it is my confident hope that it become a *vade mecum* for any future developers of the mentor concept. The book deserves to be translated into other languages to give the knowledge and experience it contains as wide an audience as possible.

Well done to Brian and Vincent for caring enough and for taking the time to leave this knowledge and experience for posterity.

Dan Flinter
Chief Executive, Enterprise Ireland

PREFACE

Towards the end of 1988, I had just retired from active professional life for the second time when I received an invitation from the Irish Industrial Development Authority, asking me to set up a Mentor Programme aimed at assisting small and medium-sized enterprises to overcome obstacles to growth. This promised to be an interesting and worthwhile assignment, so I accepted.

My first task was to recruit a small coterie of like-minded friends to help launch the idea. This initial group of 20 covered a wide range of skills and expertise and was subsequently augmented by new recruits, among them my co-author, Vincent O Neill, whom I had worked with for very many years.

Our brief from the IDA was based on the premise that we would probably help about 50 to 100 firms and that our involvement would be limited to a period of about a half-day per week. That we believed this estimate says a lot for our naiveté in the assessment of the potential demand for this service.

It quickly became apparent that the need for mentors amongst small businesses was enormous and the task was significantly greater than was first envisaged. Nothing daunted, we set out from what was essentially a "Base Camp One" to climb the heights and to set up what has become a role model for mentoring small business on a properly structured basis.

The programme grew quickly; within a few years, the panel of mentors reached 200 and the number of companies helped exceeded 2,000. We divided the country amongst a group of local regional co-ordinators. This has proved to be a key factor in the success of the programme, ensuring that the vital matching of mentors to firms is carried out at a local level.

We continued to expand our activity and received support and sponsorship from AIB. From some pretty basic initial systems, we have now developed, with the support of Enterprise Ireland, a fully integrated online web-based database and reporting system. In 2001, we carried out our 5,000th assignment.

Vincent and I wrote this book, not only for those who propose to set up a Mentor Programme, but, more importantly, to be of assistance both to mentors and potential mentorees. The **Introduction** suggests which chapters should be of most benefit to each category of reader. We have sought to provide an understanding of the relationships between mentors and those they seek to help. We have particularly emphasised the importance of trust and have tried to illustrate how mutual trust can be used to achieve a very wide range of satisfying results.

We hope that this book will help the reader to avoid a few of the many "potholes" we encountered along the way and so make the mentor's journey with the mentoree move more smoothly and quickly towards the desired goal.

I would like to thank all those we have worked with in developing mentoring in Ireland: Mike Feeney of Enterprise Ireland and Brendan Reville of the Boardroom Centre who had the original idea; Michelle Lawlor, who together with Mary Halpin of Enterprise Ireland were most supportive administrators and valued colleagues; John Kelly of AIB Bank for his confidence and generous sponsorship; our Board of Directors, particularly our first Chairman, Dr J.C. McGough, who has been my mentor. To the management and staff of Enterprise Ireland, the County Enterprise Boards and other state agencies, I extend a special word of thanks for their enthusiastic use of the Mentor Programme. Thank you very specially also to the large panel of mentors for giving so generously of their time, energy and experience. Most important of all, for me, thank you to my wife Kay for her patience, understanding and unshakeable belief that the project was worthwhile and would succeed.

Good luck to all who read this book, whether they be potential mentors, mentorees or simply have an interest in the concept of mentoring. May I wish you every success and may you have a lot of fun along the way.

Brian Doyle

INTRODUCTION

In this book, we provide:

- A list of characteristics possessed by the ideal mentor

- A survey of the likely attitudes of mentorees

- An overview of the interplay between mentor and mentoree

- Examples of two assignment meetings written in conversational form, based on the experiences of the authors

- A suggested organisational structure for a mentor programme

- Notes on the selection and training of mentors

- Guidance on the assessment of a mentoring assignment

- A Code of Conduct for mentors.

OVERVIEW OF CHAPTERS

In *Chapter 1*, we give an outline of the nature and background of mentoring. The chapter also summarises the many aspects of mentoring.

The mentor, his/her age, experience, training, qualifications, characteristics and essential approaches are considered in *Chapter 2*. We are aware that not all readers will agree with all of our views expressed on these subjects.

Chapter 3 discusses the mentoree, his reasons for seeking a mentor, the benefits of doing so and the characteristics he expects in a mentor. What a mentor expects from a mentoree is also considered.

Chapter 4 examines the relationship between the mentor and the mentoree.

An example of a first meeting of a mentoring assignment is given in **Chapter 5**. The purpose of this meeting is to familiarise the mentor with the mentoree and his business.

Chapter 6 continues the mentoring assignment by giving an example of a second meeting. More material is contained in this chapter than, perhaps, would be included in an actual second meeting.

Chapter 7 sets out in some detail the requirements for a mentoring organisation. A management structure is suggested both for a start-up mentoring entity and for a fully developed mentoring programme. The physical and financial resources required are also discussed.

Chapter 8 deals with the recruitment and training/induction of mentors. The transformation from leader to guide requires a change, not only of outlook, but also of approach. Hence the use of the word "training" as well as the word "induction".

The crucial task of assessing a completed mentoring assignment is considered in **Chapter 9**. An assessment form is introduced and is printed in full.

Chapter 10, titled *Quo Vadis Mentoring?*, recognises that everything changes and that mentoring is no different in this regard. We endeavour to look into the crystal ball.

In **Chapter 11**, the history of mentoring in literature is touched on, to give a sense of the maturity of the mentoring function. From the magical mentoring in Homer's *Odyssey* to the pragmatism of Cox and Stevens' *Selling the Wheel*, mentoring has undergone major changes over the centuries.

The **Appendix** provides a **Code of Conduct** for mentors.

HOW TO USE THIS BOOK

Readers who wish to get a quick appreciation of a mentor assignment are recommended to read **Chapter 1** first and then **Chapters 5** and **6**.

To those contemplating setting up a Mentor Programme, **Chapters 7**, **8**, **9** and the **Code of Conduct** may seem more directly relevant.

Chapters 2, **3**, **4** and **8** are included to provoke debate as we feel the subject matter is still, and is likely to remain, a developing topic.

Chapter 10 takes a tentative step into the future, while we hope that **Chapter 11** and its historical content will provide entertaining and rewarding reading.

A final note: Throughout this book, we have referred to both mentors and mentorees as "he". No significance should be read into this usage, other than a desire to spare the reader the clumsiness of "he/she" throughout.

1

THE MENTORING CONCEPT

THE PURPOSE OF MENTORING

The purpose of mentoring is to share wisdom gained from experience and learning.

An entrepreneur seeks a mentor because he is aware of some lack in his knowledge, skill or experience. His sense of inadequacy or incompleteness may have arisen because he is unsatisfied with the general progress of his business. He may feel that he is not realising its potential. It may be, on the other hand, that he seeks stability or a sense of continuity, which outside supportive intervention will provide.

Another reason for seeking a mentor is the alleviation of the loneliness and isolation of the entrepreneur.

The introduction of a mentor should support and strengthen the entrepreneur rather than create a contrast.

THE NATURE OF MENTORING

Mentoring is distinguished from advising, counselling, coaching and training:

- **Advising** is directed at helping the subject decide on a course of action.

- **Counselling** deals with particular aspects of performance, personality or career in a non-judgemental way. It has been defined as a non-directive process (the counsellor does not advise or suggest a specific course of action) by which a counsellor helps an individual to overcome problems or come to terms with feelings. He sees what options are open and chooses between them by tapping into their own inner resources.[1] It is a neutral process. Some people see mentoring as a subsection of counselling when it refers to short-term counselling.

- **Coaching** involves teaching specific skills, training in those skills and monitoring subsequent performance with a view to improving those skills. The term is usually applied to training in the sporting world.

- **Training**, a term more common in the commercial sphere, is directed at improving skills and comprises instruction, demonstration and supervision.

- **Mentoring entrepreneurs** deals with management and business processes. It involves vision (referring to a future state better than the present), mission (the timeless nature and purpose of an enterprise), listening and debating. But mentors do not have all the answers. That is why a mentor's focus is on asking questions to assist and challenge the entrepreneur in his journey of discovery.

Mentoring entrepreneurs is different from mentoring junior employees in a business, which is more in the nature of counselling or coaching.

A mentoring assignment should provide the mentoree with a greater sense of mission and give more enjoyment in work, in addition to other benefits.

Listening

> *"In conversation, one should attend closely to what is being said. And in every impulse, attend to what arises from it; in the latter case, to see from the first what end is in view, and in the former, to keep a careful watch on what people are meaning to say."*[2]

---

[1] Milne, A.R., *Counselling at Work*, CEPEC, Bromley, 1988.

[2] Marcus Aurelius, *Meditations*.

The writer of that paragraph has succinctly summarised the elements of good listening. The listener should endeavour to understand precisely what the speaker is trying to communicate. And, from that comprehension, he knows what the speaker hopes to achieve from the exchange.

Key points include:

- **Active Listening.** Listening is the most important activity in mentoring. It is a learned skill.[3] Listening is different from hearing, which is passive. Passive hearing is epitomised by the glassy stare. Listening involves the activity of taking in information in an objective manner without drawing conclusions or making judgements.

- **No Interruptions.** A perceptive mentor waits until the mentoree stops talking before asking a question or making any comment. The mentor and mentoree cannot discuss a problem or situation or suggestion until the mentoree describes and explains it. How can a mentor ask a sensible question or make a worthwhile comment about a topic being presented, if he hasn't listened to the mentoree's exposition? It follows that the mentor must not interrupt the mentoree. At the same time, it is important for him not to ignore statements with which he disagrees. It is equally important not to interject a counter-suggestion or option while the mentoree is speaking. Let the mentoree finish his commentary. Then the mentor can tease out the mentoree's reasons for making the statement by asking questions, if, at that time, he considers it pertinent to do so. The mentor thus avoids giving the impression that he can anticipate what the mentoree is going to say.

- **Seek Clarification.** The mentoree is more likely to be impressed if the mentor seeks clarification on particular points before venturing an opinion. It shows that the mentor does not make quick judgements or jump to conclusions. The way a person uses words and phrases gives rise to different interpretations. A good listener, knowing this, interprets

---

[3] Burley-Allen, M., *Listening*, Wiley, 1995.

carefully the mentoree's initial statements. More often than not, the mentor will need clarification on, at least, a few points. And, if he is mystified by a mentoree's statement, the mentor is advised to seek elucidation, after the mentoree has finished speaking. He is then in a better position to respond to it, although he may deem it more appropriate to wait until further facts emerge.

- **No Distractions.** A good listener does not let himself become distracted. He is focused on the speaker's thoughts and body language and shows by his general attitude that he is concentrating on what the mentoree is saying. It is known that a good listener engenders trust in the speaker because he shows an interest in what he is saying. He gives the speaker confidence that something will be done and inspires a spirit of co-operation. *The mentor makes sure that his mobile phone is switched off before every mentor meeting!*

- **No Staring.** An attentive mentor looks at the mentoree when he is talking but does not stare at him. A speaker needs some form of acknowledgement that he is being heard and understood. The mentor, by looking attentively at the mentoree, is thus obviously engaged in the process of listening and encourages the mentoree, for example, by nodding his head from time to time. "He listens well who notes well what he hears."[4] It is part of the confidence-building process.

- **Note-taking.** It is generally recommended that the mentor take notes when listening to the mentoree. It ensures that points made by the mentoree are not overlooked afterwards. It is also another indication to the mentoree that the mentor is listening and is taking what he says seriously. The mentor is then able to review his notes with the mentoree and ensure that the notes made are accurate. It is advisable also to summarise the mentoree's presentation and so give the mentoree the opportunity to say whether the mentor has understood what he was saying. Note-taking also helps the

[4] Dante, *The Divine Comedy.*

mentor to avoid the temptation of immediately equating the mentoree's problems or opportunities with previous experiences of which the mentor has knowledge, simply because it is more comfortable to deal with the familiar. The mentoree's presentation may deal with an option or options with which the mentor has not had any previous experience.

- **Closed-end Questions and Open-ended Questions.** The mentor should not ask closed-end questions that confine the mentoree's reply within parameters dictated by the mentor — typically, questions that demand a "Yes/No" answer. These restrict the mentoree to answering specific points raised by the mentor. It is better to ask open-ended questions and allow the mentoree to expand his answer as he sees fit.

- **Frankness.** The mentoree may give vent to negative feelings about aspects of the mentoring assignment. These should not create resentment or make the mentor feel defensive. The mentoring process is two-way and frankness by both parties helps to achieve the agreed objectives.

- **Time-saving.** The application of listening skills by the mentor shortens the time spent on an assignment by improving his understanding of the mentoree's needs. Thus less time is spent following irrelevancies that could arise from misunderstandings.

- **Mentor's Phraseology.** The application of the mentor's listening skill also involves listening to himself. What words or phrases does the mentor use, perhaps repetitively? Is his phraseology ambiguous? Is the mentor inclined to give soliloquies? Does the mentor talk too much? Is there a beginning, a middle and an end to what he says? How much self-imaging is included?

- **Learning from Listening.** Every mentoring assignment provides the mentor with an opportunity to learn something new from the mentoree. It may be an approach to a business situation, which the mentor has not heard before. It may be a unique process in customer relations. Whatever it is, if the mentor does not listen, he will learn nothing. And, if he is seen not to listen by the mentoree, he is indicating to the mentoree that he believes that he has nothing to learn from him. In which case, it would be understandable for the mentoree to conclude that the mentoree has very little, if anything, to learn from the mentor.

> *A wise old owl lived in an oak*
> *The more he saw, the less he spoke*
> *The less he spoke, the more he heard*
> *Mentors should be like that wise old bird.*

MENTORING ASSIGNMENTS

What is a mentoring assignment? Is it a training course? Is it a consultancy project? Is it an apprenticeship system?

It is none of these, although, in some cases, it will appear to fall into one of those categories.

Objectives

The mentor and the mentoree should agree the objectives of the mentoring assignment at the start of their journey of discovery. It is important that both parties clearly understand the agreed objectives. For that reason, the objectives should be stated in writing and referred to at the beginning of each meeting during the assignment.

Mentoree's Vision

The mentoree may have developed his own vision for the business, and set it out in a business plan. This will include productivity targets, some of which may have been achieved already. The mentoree may now have as one of his objectives a wish to achieve the outstanding targets sooner. In addition, he may believe that improvements in profitability could and/or should be sought and achieved. On the other hand, his aim may be, quite simply, to attain greater job satisfaction.

Mentor's Opinion

There may be cases where the mentor is of the opinion that the mentoree's business is in a parlous state. In that event, he should be tactful when ascertaining whether the mentoree is aware of this fact. No entrepreneur wants to be told bluntly that his business is in a perilous condition. The mentor may start by asking questions to assess the extent of the mentoree's awareness of the situation, and go on from there.

Skills Required

The mentoree assumes that the mentor has a skill or skills. The skills are not listed. They may be many or few. A specific technical skill, such as financial knowledge or engineering capability, may be required for the mentoring assignment. On the other hand, a generalist skill may be called for. Most importantly, mentoring is about supporting the mentoree in his progress towards his declared objectives.

Insight or perceptiveness developed over years, from education, training, and experience of problem-solving in a business environment, are the particular qualities indispensable in the mentoring process. The mentoree cannot expect more.

Preliminary Briefing

The mentor programme director should brief the mentor about the mentoree's background and his aspirations, before the mentor undertakes an assignment. He should also ensure that the mentoree is aware of the nature of mentoring and the agreed objectives of the assignment.

The mentor should be informed about of the nature of the enterprise — whether it is a "lifestyle company", where the owner's primary motivation is to make a reasonable living, or a "growth" company, where the entrepreneur is driven by the ambition to build a business of some significance.

Mentor's Approach

The approach to be adopted by the mentor is, to a great extent, dependent on the stage of business development of the mentoree and the type of commercial experience he has had. Is the mentoree a novice in business, an apprentice entrepreneur with some experience, a partly skilled manager, or an experienced businessperson? The mentor's approach to, and nature of, the assignment is dictated in part by the answers to these questions.

Certainly, there are elements of a quasi-apprenticeship when, for example, the mentor introduces concepts with which the mentoree is unfamiliar — for example, the methodology of a marketing activity schedule, referred to in **Chapter 6**, the preparation of a projected cash flow statement, or the linkage of marketing activities to sales.

The mentor demonstrates the models of such concepts in order to answer questions raised by the mentoree or to fill an obvious gap in the management procedures.

The mentor, too, is on a learning curve. Much of what he learns on one assignment can be used in another assignment. Mentoring is yet another two-way conduit for experience.

Mentoree's Demands

What demands can the mentoree make on the mentor? Obviously the demands have to be reasonable. This caution refers to all the arrangements made for the mentoring assignment — for example:

- The times of day (and night) the mentoree can call the mentor

- The selection of the venue for the meetings

- The number of hours the mentoree can expect the mentor to spend at each meeting.

If the mentoree is regarded as the customer in the assignment, then the mentoree's wishes may be regarded as paramount. There are limits, however, as this could allow the mentoree, for example, to "think out loud" at the meetings and so waste time because he did not prepare for a meeting.

On the other hand, if the mentor is introducing new concepts to, say, an apprentice entrepreneur, he should not overload the mentoree with information at any one meeting and should allocate his time accordingly.

Length of Mentoring Assignment

Before the assignment commences, the period of time during which the mentoring process will take place needs to be discussed with the mentoree. The joint analysis of the needs of the enterprise is important in estimating the time required, as well as the success of the mentoring process.

The programme for the assignment may be divided into several phases, each phase lasting a specified time. There may be a break between one phase and the next. The break, having been agreed by both mentor and mentoree, allows time for the application of solutions or for new procedures to mature.

The time required for any assignment depends on the nature and magnitude of the agreed objectives. The objectives are influenced by the stage of development of the business.

Stage of Business Development

There are four stages of business development and they can be classified as follows:

- **Start-up:** The mentoree is establishing a new enterprise and wants help in installing appropriate management procedures.

- **Mentoree with some business experience:** He has been in business for a short period and now wants assistance in planning the next phase of expansion within the resources available.

- **Mentoree with some skill:** He feels the need for guidance in developing those skills and acquiring others.

- **Experienced businessperson:** He would welcome someone to act as a sounding board for his ideas for the further development of the business.

We have referred already, albeit briefly, to the level of knowledge and experience the new mentoree may have had and how it influences the mentor's approach; for example:

- **Start-up:** In a start-up, the mentoree may have some knowledge and/or skill in the industry or may be a complete novice. The level of the mentoree's familiarity with the industry largely dictates the mentoring approach. It is essential to remember that mentoring does not encompass becoming a quasi-joint entrepreneur. Guidance is what is required. In this type of case, a somewhat prolonged mentoring assignment is appropriate.

- **Mentoree with some business experience:** The mentoree is capable of articulating the areas where he requires assistance. The mentoring required is, probably, of a specialist nature and is supportive and motivational. The nature of the specialisation will largely dictate the time period seen as necessary.

- **Mentoree with some skill:** The mentoree has progressed the business some distance and needs reinforcement of confidence and an element of "Where to now?" discussion. This type of assignment can be extremely time-consuming, as the mentoree may not have prepared more than the question.

- **Experienced businessperson:** The mentoree is very experienced and seeks to talk to a seasoned businessperson about his ideas and to probe a fresh outlook brought to bear on his business. From the mentoring, he hopes to develop the business in a more dynamic and, possibly, a broader way. The time for this type of assignment need not be too extended.

Number of Mentors

A mentoring assignment is not, necessarily, restricted to one mentor. Several mentors may be appointed to the enterprise to provide knowledge in various areas. It is generally better if only one mentor is acting at any one time. There are occasions, however, when it is beneficial to have more than one mentor at the same time to ensure co-ordination when the spheres of their assignments are interrelated.

Mentoree to become a Mentor?

Mentoring should be enjoyable to both mentor and mentoree. In time, there is the possibility that the mentoree may, himself, become a mentor to other entrepreneurs. Chapter 8 looks at this possibility in more detail.

MENTORING MEETINGS

Mentoring meetings are usually one-to-one. Some entrepreneurs, however, like to involve colleagues or staff in some or all of the mentor visits. When this happens, faster progress towards achievement of the agreed objectives can, sometimes, be made. The staff members concerned usually provide a different perception of a problem or process and may add extra scenarios from which a solution is selected. Furthermore, the inclusion of staff members in the meetings may provide an insight into staff relations within the business.

Video of Meetings

It might be worth considering recording mentor visits on video, with the aim of extending the benefits to a wider audience within the business. This wider involvement can, on occasion, be useful because it gives others working in the business an understanding of the purpose of the mentor assignment and the operation of the mentoring process.

The video will highlight the goals of the business and will show the linkage between the viewer's work and the work of other staff members. It will demonstrate how their joint and several contributions towards the achievement of those goals advance the enterprise as a result.

The use of videos, however, should be seen as an add-on and not as a substitute for face-to-face mentoring. Mentoring is devoted to guidance, following discussion, in tackling problems identified by the mentoree and, of necessity, involves personal encounter.

Timing of Meetings

The timing and regularity of the mentor/mentoree meetings should be agreed at the beginning of the assignment.

Some entrepreneurs favour early morning meetings before business activity commences, with its inevitable interruptions. Others prefer to meet at lunchtime, others after business hours.

Inevitably, some discussions will have to take place during business hours because the developments, processes or problems under consideration occur when the undertaking is functioning and should be seen in operation by the mentor.

Meetings between mentor and mentoree, if they are to achieve their ideals, should, in so far as is possible, occur at agreed fixed intervals. The length of the intervals depends on the objectives of the mentoring assignment and the time schedules of both parties. Four to six weeks seems to be the norm.

Length of Meetings

The length of the mentor meetings can vary. Not all meetings can be programmed to last a specified time, however desirable that may be. Those involved in the discussions may decide that consideration of developments should be the subject of some meetings and reviews of processes be the subject of others, or that all matters currently being examined be dealt with at each meeting. Crisis issues often demand more time. For example, the planning process is time-consuming and cannot be foreshortened.

Holding regular meetings is more important than setting time limits for the duration of the meetings.

Location of Meetings

Where possible, mentoring should be carried out in the entrepreneur's business premises. That way, the mentor gains greater familiarity with the workings of the enterprise and can better understand the reasons for questions raised by the mentoree.

Nonetheless, there are times when it is more beneficial to mentor in an off-site location. The advantages are:

- Lack of distraction by the day-to-day demands of the business

- Greater ability to take an overview of the business in unassociated surroundings

- Relative ease of concentration when confronting problems away from the pressures they create.

However, off-site, the mentor is dependent on the mentoree's memory, descriptive ability, verbal fluency, honesty, integrity of purpose and ability to visualise the workplace.

Structure of Meetings

Mentoring entrepreneurs has to be on a structured basis. This does not mean that the meetings have to be rigidly formal. Some informality, in any friendly relationship, is to be expected. There are times, of course, when formality is more appropriate.

The structural element in the mentor meetings ensures that the agreed objectives are discussed regularly. For this reason, an agenda is recommended. Examples of agendas for the first and second mentor meetings are included in *Chapters 5* and *6*.

The entrepreneur must understand that mentoring is not a panacea for all his problems. The purpose of mentoring is to stimulate the entrepreneur to consider the possibilities available to him and to provoke a debate about the options available. Mentoring will not necessarily save the enterprise, if that, indeed, is the objective.

ENDING THE ASSIGNMENT

What happens when the mentoring assignment ends? The end of an assignment should involve:

- A debriefing

- The possibility of future reviews

- Disengagement.

Debriefing

A form of debriefing is essential. If the mentor was assigned by a mentor programme, whether semi-state or private enterprise, a review of the progress of the assignment, its stated objectives and its achievements should be made. The same applies if the mentor appointment was by mutual consent between the mentor and mentoree.

The review should be in two parts, covering both the opinion of the mentor and the opinion of the mentoree. Where there are material differences in the views expressed, a reconciliation of the facts, as seen by both parties, needs to be made. This is dealt with in more detail in *Chapter 9*.

It may be that fundamentally irreconcilable approaches to the assignment will be uncovered. It is trite to say that these should have been identified at an early stage of the assignment. However, we should remember the old adage that "perfection is always over the horizon".

Future Reviews

Where both parties regard the mentor assignment as having made a worthwhile contribution to the enterprise, the mentor and mentoree may arrange to meet a few times a year thereafter to discuss developments since the assignment ended.

Disengagement

At the same time, it is important that the mentoree should not have developed a dependence on the mentor. Evidence of dependence would suggest that the mentor had departed from his role as guide and had become involved in management. This is contrary to the concept of a mentoring process.

It is one of the attributes of a successful mentoring assignment that the mentor can disengage from the mentoree when the assignment ends without any trauma for the mentoree.

2

THE MENTOR

WHAT IS A MENTOR?

A mentor is many things, including:

* Friend

* Philosopher

* Guide.

Friend

The first hurdle the mentor and mentoree have to surmount is one of compatibility. In spite of careful matching of the mentor and mentoree by the mentor programme director, there is always the possibility of a mismatch between the mentor and the mentoree.

Our definition of mentor is: guide, philosopher and friend. Perhaps it should be friend, guide and philosopher.

A business friendship, between the mentor and the mentoree, based on trust is essential. Without it, the mentoring assignment will not achieve the best result.

Do not expect an instant rapport. To start with, there will be mutual evaluation, but whether there is a prospect of a business friendship, founded on mutual respect, will be apparent quickly.

If the mentor and mentoree cannot be business friends, as distinct from social friends, it is better to terminate the assignment tactfully but immediately.

Philosopher

> *"A 'philo-sopher' really means 'one who loves wisdom'*
> *... A philosopher knows that in reality he knows very lit-*
> *tle. That is why he constantly strives to achieve true in-*
> *sight."*[5]

Armed with this insight, the mentor is naturally humble. In mentoring, the mentor is increasing his knowledge and experience. These enable comparison with previous experiences, identifying similarities and differences and avoiding any tendency to jump to conclusions.

Not all entrepreneurs are confident about their ability to succeed in their chosen enterprise. Nevertheless, they are rarely impressed by a mentor who gives the impression that he has all the answers instantaneously. Entrepreneurs are more likely to take seriously a mentor who gives consideration to their questions, and expresses an opinion or, on occasion, confesses that the topic is outside their knowledge or experience.

Even entrepreneurs who are confident in their own ability to succeed will, at times, suffer moments of doubt or insecurity. The mentor must be sensitive towards such anxieties and uncertainties, which most entrepreneurs experience. But, if these doubts are forming a blockage to the progress of the mentoring assignment, it is important for the mentor to question and probe, to achieve insight into those uncertainties, so that they do not hinder progress.

Guide

The mentoree's nature, expertise, values, motivation, ability to achieve and ambition to succeed at his business, all temper the mentor's approach.

The mentoree must not expect the mentor to tell or instruct him what to do, how to do it and when to do it. That would be a denial of the role of mentor.

---

[5] Gaarder, Jostein, *Sophie's World*, Phoenix House, 1995.

The mentor's role is not a form of instruction. But it is more than a counselling or training role. It is a shared mentoring experience with a guide, philosopher and friend.

It cannot be too often stated that the mentoree is not the only person to benefit from the mentoring experience. The mentor also learns from the encounter: more knowledge, additional experience, more examples of industrial norms, and increased awareness of decisions made in circumstances similar to or different from others already experienced, all of which can be used in other mentor assignments. The mentor's awareness of this learning benefit promotes a humility, which should encourage the mentoree to be forthcoming in his discussions.

WHAT DOES MENTORING INVOLVE?

Values

Mentoring is concerned with values. It is impossible for a mentor to work with an entrepreneur whose values are different, or even opposed, to his own. If there are minor or subtle differences in values, the gap between them may be bridged with discussion. Where the values are incompatible, the mentor must withdraw from the assignment.

The values in question are, for example, compliance with the law, honesty, treatment of employees, customer relations, and social attitude. The mentor should adhere to the Code of Conduct (see *Appendix*).

Role-modelling

Does role-modelling play a part? In this activity, the mentor and mentoree assume opposed roles on either side of a disputed process. It is usually advantageous if the mentor espouses the mentoree's solution and persuades the mentoree to attempt to disprove the mentor's adopted solution. The procedure is closely allied to war games that lay out a set of imaginary circumstances while the contestants endeavour to take advantage of those circumstances to benefit themselves.

Role-modelling is a useful method of highlighting problems and stimulating the consideration of available options. It impels both parties to examine a situation from disparate points of view. It is also an effective way of introducing a possibly unpalatable conclusion to a mentoree.

Goals of Mentoring

The goals of a mentoring assignment should be agreed at the beginning of the process. By beginning is meant after an assessment by the mentor of the business and its stage of development. Note that the mentoree's view of the business's need may differ from that of the mentor.

The mentoree sought the help of the mentor to solve perceived problems. The mentor may disagree with the mentoree's view of the primary needs of the enterprise. A discussion about the priorities of the mentoring assignment is then essential. For example, the mentor may think that the business needs capital, or lacks sufficient growth, or is deficient in the management of cash flow. The mentoree may disagree and be hell-bent on expansion, without considering the consequences of over-trading. To proceed without resolving such a significant difference in point of view would be disastrous.

Cultural Differences

How significant are differences across the social divide between mentor and mentoree? It seems obvious that extreme imbalance in education and culture contrast should be avoided. Sensitivity in dealing with any such contrast is a major part of mentor orientation.

These differences, if handled tactfully, need not be a barrier to communication. If they are, the mentor should withdraw tactfully and suggest a substitute mentor. On the other hand, they can be viewed as providing a potential advantage, bringing imaginative freshness from the diversity of background and outlook.

Where there appear to be irreconcilable differences, the mentor and mentoree should agree to differ, and part.

Concept of Excellence

The mentor helps the mentoree to develop a concept of excellence. This should be a continuous theme in the mentoring process. It is important that the mentoree is made aware of the desirability of striving for excellence, in every aspect of his business. There are many business excellence models available and the mentor should be able to introduce the mentoree to some of them.

Every business is expected to have a sense of community responsibility and respect for the environment and the mentor will include these principles in the pursuit of excellence. It does not have to be pressed on a reluctant mentoree, but it ought to be taken as accepted that the business will be managed with due regard to the environmental requirements of its location and best business and social practices.

A respect for the laws of the land is part of the mentor's make-up and it is important that the mentoree is aware of this and shares that respect. That is not to suggest that the mentoree does not have the same respect but it must be seen as a component of the traits of a mentor.

A shared vision of change is invaluable. Today, this could be seen as necessary as the pace of change is accelerating. It is unlikely that the mentoree is unaware of it, particularly in his own business. How the changes impact on his business is relevant material for discussion. And quantification of the likely consequences for the business from inevitable change is essential when evaluating the realism of targets set.

The mentor assists the mentoree in the development of objectives — the What. He stimulates the dedication to goal achievement — the How. With observance of good social practice, both are encompassed in the pursuit of excellence.

Mentor's Career to Date

The mentor must have enjoyed at least a modicum of success in his business career. The definition of success in the context of a qualification for mentoring is difficult.

It is well-known that few people have been blessed with continuous success. The average businessman or professional will have made mistakes. Of themselves, these can be learning experiences, albeit unpleasant ones.

The ability to cope with the consequences of the mistakes is, however, of relevance. And it is not simply a question of correcting the mistakes. Some situations are irretrievable and the ability to recognise them as such is of value.

In evaluating the career of a businessperson, one examines the overall trend. The successful trend we speak of, if drawn on a graph, would show an upward trend line. It is unlikely that the trend line will be a straight line rising ever upward. There will be, more likely than not, several blips down and up again, similar to the trend line of a share price.

What are the characteristics of success? Is it money, human relations, quality of life, doing good deeds for the community, or being popular? It is all of these things, woven into a lifestyle fabric.

It is easier to state what is *not* the kind of success appropriate to a mentor. A lifestyle dependant on professional gambling, a business career relying on pulling strokes, a reputation of continuous strife with trade unions are not qualities sought in a mentor.

The mentor is expected to be mature, practical, and congenial. The mentor must be a just person.

THE ROLE OF THE MENTOR

A question often asked is whether the role of the mentor is diagnostic or dynamic — dynamic in the sense of being active technically, applying common sense or, perhaps, something more. The answer is not easy because the mentor brings a complex set of skills to an assignment. It is this range of skills that we consider here.

What a mentor does changes from assignment to assignment. This may seem strange at first mention, because public perceptions of professional roles tend to be essentially generic: a doctor makes his patients well again, a solicitor works in the law courts, an accountant prepares accounts, and so on. We know, of course, that those perceptions are outrageously narrow. So it is with mentoring.

General

A mentor presents the big picture. His tasks are more general, because he is not familiar with the detail of the mentoree's business.

He may bring a specialist skill.

He is, usually, future-oriented. He discusses and, jointly with the mentoree, assesses future potential. The mentor's views and the views of the mentoree of what the future holds will, possibly, differ and the opinion of the mentor is not necessarily the one that prevails. Even with such a detailed review, the possibility of error is always present. Economic booms and slumps are cyclical. So too are the ups and downs of a business, not necessarily in line with economic cycles. The mentor assignment can commence at the start, in the middle or at the end of either. It doesn't matter when. The mentor and mentoree are on a mutual quest to select the right aim and to achieve it. They are involved in a search together.

The mentor convinces by his presence that he has belief in the mentoree's ability to achieve his goals. It will be obvious to the mentoree that, if the mentor did not have that confidence, he would not continue with the mentoring assignment.

The mentor should be visible. He should actually spend time at reasonable intervals in the mentoree's premises. This does not preclude meetings off the mentoree's premises. The location and timing of the meetings is agreed between them.

The mentor must be accessible. It should be possible for the mentoree to make contact with the mentor at all reasonable times.

Mentor Activity

Mentoring is active:

* The mentor must be **competent**. He must have a transferable skill that is relevant to the mentoree's needs and is up-to-date. The mentor's skill has been acquired by study, training, experience and regular attendance at courses. And he must demonstrate this competence in his mentoring assignments. Not only must the mentor have the ability to ap-

ply the acquired skill, he must also have the discipline to apply the skill gained.

- The mentor should be an **eager learner** and ask for specifics. This questioning approach stimulates the mentoree to clarify his thinking — something the average mentoree rarely has time to do. The mentor expects to learn from the mentoree about his business and general commercial matters. In turn, he passes what he has learned from one mentoree, provided that it is not confidential, to another mentoree.

- The mentor is **opportunistic** in a positive way. He is well-read and takes advantage of opportunities in a non-threatening way. The mentor is a professional and, like good professionals, he will keep up-to-date in all topics relevant to his profession. He is competent to apply principles and aphorisms from one discipline to another.

The mentor is aware of the mutual win — the mentor **wants to learn** too. Mutual learning is the key. Asking for explanations from the mentoree about courses of action contemplated is not necessarily seeking justification. It can be a desire to add to the mentor's store of knowledge. And it is a good idea to let the mentoree know the reason for the question. It underlines for the mentoree the genuineness of the mentor's statement at the commencement of the mentoring assignment that the search for knowledge is a joint activity. The reference to the two-way flow of information in the mentoring process can be repeated several times during the assignment.

Analysis

The mentor has to fully understand the assignment.

1. What does the mentoree **want**?

2. What does the mentoree **need**?

3. What is the **mentoree's perception of his needs**?

4. How does his perception compare with the **mentor's perception of his needs**?

The reconciliation of the answers to these four questions is the starting point for the mentor's activity in the assignment.

In every mentoring assignment, the mentor does not know what will confront him when he makes his first visit to the entrepreneur's premises.

He will have had a preliminary briefing from the programme director but, for practical reasons, that will not have been comprehensive, because the director does not have the time to do an in-depth examination of the mentoree's needs — perhaps no more than to listen to the mentoree's statement of his objectives and note them for transmission to the mentor. Thus the preliminary briefing given by the director to the mentor provides only an outline of the objectives of the mentoring assignment.

The mentor's detailed examination of the business with the mentoree may confirm the briefing content received from the co-ordinator or expand it.

There is also the possibility that the mentor's perception of the needs of the mentoree will be different from those of the director. It may be that the mentor's view may even differ from that of the mentoree. What to do then? The mentor, as stated previously, listens and asks questions with a view to achieving consensus on the goals of the assignment. The question-and-answer sessions that follow may be long and arduous but they cannot be avoided.

If the mentor assignment is aimed at making a specific decision on the future direction of the business, for example, the mentor can ask the mentoree to list the sources of information that are available, and to identify those he has consulted to date. He can ask the mentoree to define the timeframe within which the decision must be made and within which goal achievement is planned — each step must be defined and scheduled. He can then ask him if the data he has collected confirm or suggest that the options he is considering can be achieved within the planned timeframe. The objective of this process is to reduce the possibility of a hasty decision.

To proceed on the basis of different viewpoints about the aims to be pursued would make the assignment nugatory. And, if agreement cannot be reached on the mentoree's needs, the mentor should withdraw from the assignment.

Listening and Questioning

The mentor encourages the exploration of options by asking questions. It is important to make clear to the mentoree that the questions do not imply criticism of the mentoree's opinions. The questions should be phrased to encourage the exploration in depth of options proposed by the mentoree. Indeed, they may lead to the discovery of other options, not previously thought of, which can now be considered. The mentor always keeps in the forefront of his mind that it is the mentoree who makes the decisions about what courses of action are to be followed to achieve the agreed objectives.

The use of the word "Why?" is one of the best ways of provoking detailed examination of a proposed course of action. The question may be asked even when the mentor agrees with the mentoree's conclusion in a particular circumstance.

This questioning method is adopted at all times in the mentoring process to help engender a logical approach to decision-making. It is a methodology that the mentoree may well come to value above all else.

When the objectives of the mentoring assignment are agreed, the next question to ask the mentoree is "Does he wish the mentor to be his guide in the search for the way to achieve his goals?" The sequence of these two questions ("What are the goals?" and "Do you want me involved?") is important. Some times, a mentor is tempted to seek the answer to the second question first, perhaps as a reassurance.

Searching

At all times during the assignment, the mentor searches for the capabilities and potential of the mentoree and the possibilities available to him. It can be a shared search, in which both mentor and mentoree participate, staying within their roles, and providing support and strength to the eventual conclusion. The mentor helps develop the mentoree's drive in proportion to his personal capacity for it. There is little point to developing un-reasonable expectations in the mentoree.

The focus is always on the number and nature of options available to the mentoree. The search for the choice of the right option is the task both parties are engaged in. That is certainly the aspiration of the mentoring process. The concept of a jour-ney, a quest, a search is ever-present in mentoring. A mentor, by participating in the journey, helps the mentoree to improve — to "move on".

The mentoree's drive supports venturesome risk-taking ac-tion. It is the function of the mentor to join the mentoree in the search for a practical and common-sense approach to the risks being undertaken. The mentor is reminded that risk-taking is not synonymous with recklessness; nor, on the other hand, should the mentoree be encouraged to assume that risk-taking automatically entitles him to gain a profit from it.

The mentor and the mentoree share the search. The men-toree always makes the ultimate choice. Both mentor and men-toree know that decision-making is fraught with uncertainty (and it may be no harm to mention it), because of the lack of comprehensive information and insufficient time to give ade-quate consideration to the data that is available. How can the mentor help?

The mentor helps the mentoree's awareness of issues. If the mentor perceives that the mentoree is taking the line of least resistance, he will bring to his attention other issues and their likely influence by asking pertinent questions so that the men-toree can use his talents to their full potential.

Supporting

If, in the mentor's view, the mentoree is about to make a hasty decision, because of perceived pressures on him to do so, as his guide, the mentor's support and calm demeanour in the pe-riod of adversity may encourage the mentoree to pause for mature consideration — perhaps simply by asking whether there are reasons for pause to take stock of all the possibilities before making decisions.

A positive attitude, however, is indispensable when facing adversity and the use of encouraging words and phrases are preferable to noncommittal or negative statements, without appearing to advocate complacency. The mentoree should be supported at all times and the mentor's approach can influence the mentoree's response to challenges.

WHAT THE MENTOR'S ROLE IS NOT

It should be equally clear what the mentor's role is not:

- Mentors should not see their role as one of **criticism**, even if it is constructive criticism.

- Nor is it the function of a mentor to **assess the performance** of the mentoree or give judgement on his achievement. Bearing in mind that the fundamental role of the mentor is to guide the mentoree towards improving his business by asking questions, it follows that judgement, if judgement is to be made, is the province of the mentoree. The objective of the mentoring process is to help the mentoree make decisions that will progress him towards the achievement of his goals.

- The mentor's role is not one of **rescue**. This last statement is, probably, the most difficult for many mentors to accept because there is always the temptation to "roll up one's sleeves" and get involved. But what is the mentor to do if the picture presented on his first visit is one of unrelieved gloom? What if the business is in need of rescue? For one thing, there are business rescue specialists and the mentoree may be well-advised to consult one.

- The mentor is not in any position to **provide a quick fix**, nor should he attempt to do so. A mentor wants the mentoree to achieve his objectives by pursuing them in a responsible manner over a reasonably extended period of time — say, three to five years. He may assist the mentoree, however, to find a temporary solution to an existing problem. It will be understood, hopefully, by both parties that it is just that, a temporary solution, and that the search for a permanent resolution should be continued.

- He is not the **decision-maker**. One can never repeat too often that it is the mentoree who makes the decisions. The mentor's role is to act as confidant, guide and sponsor, to help the mentoree to realise the potential of his business. The mentor is a steadying influence.

MENTOR CHARACTERISTICS

The characteristics of a successful mentor include:

- Abilities

- Qualities

- Attitudes

- Ethics/Values.

Abilities

- **Listening Skills.** The mentor listens, *listens*, **listens** . . . and then speaks. The mentor listens attentively and does not interrupt the mentoree. To clarify a point, however, the mentor, when occasion permits, may ask a question. This cycle is repeated throughout the assignment. Sometimes, the mentoree's clear articulation of a problem to another person suggests the solution. Simply by listening carefully to the mentoree in his examination of a problem, the mentor may help him to find the solution.

- **Asking Questions.** On occasion, the mentor takes the initiative and asks questions. He guides by asking questions. It is the application of the method used by Socrates to guide by asking questions. Ask "Why?", the most potent question. The mentoree must then rationalise. Can he justify his suggested solution to a problem and/or planned course of action? It is the mentor's function to seek answers from the mentoree. Without them, the mentor cannot achieve his mentoring goal of guidance. The information in the answers provided by the mentoree should be put in a measurable format. Without a metric, it is not possible to monitor progress or improvement.

- **Leadership.** The mentor leads by example. To do so, he should have skills appropriate to the assignment. Apart from the technical skill(s) the mentor possesses, he must also have specific mentoring skills. Added to these, he must have the ability to exercise those skills, and the discipline to apply them. The mentoree, too, has a skill or skills. The mentoring process assumes that the mentoree is able to apply his skills. The question then is, "Does the mentoree have the requisite discipline to do so in order to achieve his objectives?" By exercising his mentoring skills, the mentor helps the mentoree to find his own way through business problems and to progress towards fulfilling his potential.

- **Ability to Empower.** The mentor's function is to empower the mentoree. Mentor and mentoree are equals. The mentor assists, but the mentoree is the doer. The mentor should tell the mentoree what he, the mentor, hopes to get from the assignment. The mentoree should be encouraged to do likewise. The articulation of expectations, hopefully mutual expectations, aids understanding and may avoid disappointments later. It underlines inclusiveness.

- **Ability to Network.** Sometimes the mentor may see the benefit to the mentoree of networking by the mentor. This may present the mentor with a dilemma. If the mentor is not supposed to be "hands-on", how can he network on behalf of the mentoree? One can argue that networking is hardly "hands-on" and, in any event, it is not a case of taking over the decision-making process. Furthermore, the mentor does not wish to appear unduly rigid in the application of the "no hands-on" principle. Introducing the mentoree to someone who might be helpful to him does not damage the perception of a mentor guiding by listening and questioning.

- **Empathy.** There must be empathy with the mentoree. This returns us to the question of a business friendship and the mutual trust that is fundamental to a productive mentor assignment.

Qualities

- **Experience.** The mentor should have experience appropriate to the assignment. This is self-evident. If the mentoring assignment is about a production problem, it is probably pointless to assign a marketing mentor to the business. By means of the mentoring techniques discussed, the mentor provides information to the mentoree. The information is appropriate, compact, comprehensible, and capable of application.

- **Passion and Enthusiasm.** The true mentor is passionate and enthusiastic. The pursuit of excellence is challenging in any field. The mentor can demonstrate in his approach a belief that the mentoree is as excited about the search for excellence as the mentor is.

- **Time Efficiency.** The mentor devotes attention, time, diligence, and skill to each assignment. The mentoree will be appreciative of the time spent with him by the mentor. The mentor, while devoting sufficient time to achieve his purpose, will not be wasteful of his time or mentoree's. Husbanding of time is a skill in itself and it is beneficial if the mentoree is aware that it is a skill like any other. A mentor should be punctual. He should be time-efficient (remember the mentoree has a business to manage). The question may be asked, "Are mentors selected because they have skills or because they have time?" Of course, they must have both. Without skill and the time in which to share it with the mentoree, the mentor is inoperative.

- **Sense of Humour.** A mentor must have a sense of humour. No matter how serious the problems are, a sense of humour is never out of place. Tact and sensitivity in the use of humour, however, are essential.

- **Capacity for Enjoyment.** Mentoring should be enjoyable. Helping an entrepreneur to achieve his objectives provides satisfaction. The mentor is not part of the business and he does not have a financial interest in any outcome. His job satisfaction derives from the mentoree's success.

- **A Sense of Equality.** The mentor must not speak down to the mentoree. Fundamental to the mentoring relationship is equality between the mentor and mentoree. Communication must be at the same level. Hence the earlier reference to equivalent lifestyles.

- **Ethical Conduct.** The mentor is ethical. What mentor would expect to be otherwise? The *Appendix* contains a *Code of Conduct* for mentors.

- **Humility.** The mentor should approach every assignment with humility. It is salutary for the mentor to reflect on what his attitude would be if he were confronted with a particular problem facing the mentoree. While the mentor provides a service to the mentoree combining skill, knowledge and commercial experience, as mentioned previously, this does not imply that the mentor is expected to be infallible. The accepted presumption is that the mentor has considerable commercial experience. The mentor must have skill in some aspect of business, whether it is very specialist such as software engineering or more general expertise such as marketing, production, finance, or general management. It follows that the mentor must not be arrogant. Any hint of arrogance on the part of the mentor will be disastrous to the mentoring relationship. As stated previously, the mentoring process is two-way. The mentor learns from the mentoree, too, whether simply facts about the mentoree's industry or cutting-edge information on management techniques.

Attitudes

- **Respect for the Mentoree.** The complete mentor will show respect for the mentoree, both as a person and the provider of knowledge and the mentor's companion in the search for excellence in his business. And he will acknowledge to the mentoree the receipt of enlightenment on matters arising in the process.

- **Willingness to Take Criticism.** Expectations from the mentoring assignment are likely to be the first set of negotiations between the parties. Regular reviews of progress, with appropriate measurements, towards the agreed goals of the mentoring assignment should be made jointly. If the mentoree is unhappy with the progress of the assignment or of the methodology adopted by the mentor, he should be encouraged to say so.

- **Honesty.** The mentor is manifestly honest. The mentor must be seen to be an honest person. This fits neatly with his sense of justice. It also complements his respect for the law and the community.

- **Caring.** The mentor is caring. What distinguishes the thoughtful mentor is his willingness to care. The mentor cares about the advancement of the mentoree. He is dedicated to share the search for the "What?" and the "How?" of the mentoree's business. Genuineness in pursuing the search is vital in demonstrating to the mentoree a caring attitude for his problems and their solution.

- **Supportiveness.** The mentor provides support and strengthens the resolve of the mentoree by his presence and his interest in the mentoree's problems. He is there as a companion in the quest for improvement in the mentoree's enterprise and achievement of his goals.

Ethics/Values

- **Reporting to the Programme Director.** The mentor's objectives should accord with the mentoree's objectives and these should be in writing. He should report regularly to the Programme Director on the perceived progress of the assignment.

- **Conduct Self-Assessments.** The mentor should conduct regular self-assessments in respect of each assignment. A suggested format for such assessments is provided in *Chapter 4*.

THE FIRST MEETING

The first meeting of the mentor and mentoree can set the tone for all future meetings and, indeed, may influence the success or failure of the process, so it is imperative that it is planned in a systematic way. A suggested agenda is provided in **Chapter 5**.

To start on a good footing at that meeting, the mentor will introduce himself to the mentoree in some detail. It is recommended that the mentor will start by giving an outline of his career to date, noting his successes and not ignoring his failures.

The mentor, obviously, concentrates on the business aspects of his career, not his personal details. Academic achievements may be touched on briefly but not stressed. The mentoree may not have been academically gifted, by choice or otherwise, or may be cynical about academic honours.

The business and social status of the mentor should not be one that makes the mentoree stand in awe of the mentor. It is for these reasons that the matching of mentor and mentoree is so important, and the mentor's method of introduction is crucial because of the prerequisite that the mentor and mentoree establish good rapport from the beginning.

It must be made clear to the mentoree that the mentor does not consider himself to be anyone special, is fallible like the mentoree, and has a lifestyle which the mentoree can understand and with which he can empathise.

It can also be said that, if the mentor does not understand the environment in which the entrepreneur operates, he will find it difficult to understand the entrepreneur. That is why, during the initial familiarising meeting, the mentor seeks to learn as much as possible about all aspects of the mentoree's business and the industrial environment in which it operates. In that respect, the meeting is not too dissimilar to a doctor's first consultation with a patient.

CONCLUSION

The archetype mentor represents knowledge, reflection, insight, wisdom, cleverness, and intuition. He features where insight, understanding, good advice, determination, planning, etc. are needed but cannot be mustered on one's own, often arriving in the nick of time to help the traveller along the journey.[6]

Listening and asking questions are the supreme qualities of a mentor.

Socrates said: "Look then how he will come out of his perplexity while searching along with me. I shall do nothing more than ask questions and not teach him. Watch whether you find me teaching and explaining things to him instead of asking for his opinion."[7]

Saint Francis said, "It is in giving that we receive."

---

[6] Jung, C.J., *Psyche and Symbol*, Doubleday, New York, 1958, p. 71.

[7] Plato, *Meno*, Grube, GMA, Hackett Publishing Company Inc., 1981.

3

THE MENTOREE

The mentoree is the focal point of any and every mentoring assignment. Clearly a mentor has no function without a mentoree.

The mentor will have emphasised to the mentoree, at the start of the assignment, that the mentoring process is a journey that they will undertake together in a mutual search for the best options available and for solutions to problems encountered. The concepts of journey and search are as relevant for the mentoree as they are for the mentor.

The mentoree is provided with a confidential environment for gaining technical skills. It will be made clear to him that, although initially he may feel exposed or embarrassed in front of his staff by the presence of the mentor, the mentoring process is as private as the mentoree wishes. If he does not wish the staff to know about the mentor's involvement, the meetings can take place away from the business premises.

At this juncture, it is worthwhile, perhaps, to spend some time considering the possible motivation of a mentoree when he decides to seek and engage a mentor.

REASONS FOR SEEKING A MENTOR

Why does a mentoree feel that he needs a mentor? The following are some of the reasons that have been suggested:

- He feels that he has lost his way and needs objective assistance to guide him back on course.

- He has encountered a particular problem in his business and looks for help in solving it.

- He wants someone to talk to about his business. Managing a small business is a lonely occupation.

- He is seeking someone who will act as a sounding board for his ideas. He is aware that there are many possible routes to take, but he may have no one with whom to test his ideas.

- He wants to know how and when to decide to commit himself and his business to a course of action?

- He is not sure whether he has the resources to achieve his goals.

- He has decided to review his business with the aim of preparing a business plan for its development and needs guidance in its preparation.

- He believes that a particular process of his business is not being exploited to its maximum potential, and he needs guidance on how to take advantage of opportunities available.

What Kind of Mentor?

What kind of mentor does a mentoree need? Should the mentor be:

- A specialist in one aspect of business — for example, production, marketing, finance or human relations?

- A generalist with wide management expertise?

- A person with a deep knowledge of a particular industry?

Age of Mentor/Mentoree

What age should the mentor be? Is age relevant? Surely there must be a minimum age requirement?

Will the mentoree be surprised at the age of the mentor? Did he expect someone older or younger? Is the age difference going to be a problem? Is the language used of a different generation? If there is a problem under any of these headings, can it be overcome?

The mentoree needs an answer to these questions before engaging in the process. It is helpful if the mentor himself raises these questions with the mentoree. It is a practical example of openness and can give the mentoree confidence in the process itself. He can then discuss the issue of age with the mentor without embarrassment.

Fears of Mentoree

At the first meeting between the mentor and mentoree, the mentor tells the mentoree that mentors are as fallible as anyone else.

At the same time, the mentoree faces the prospect that his weaknesses will be exposed during the mentoring assignment. He would hope that the mentor would focus on his strengths too and not just on his weaknesses, although he will have taken that possibility into account. He takes the risk, nevertheless, because, ideally, he perceives the mentor as his guide and champion.

It cannot be easy for an entrepreneur to come face to face, in the presence of another person — in this case, the mentor — with his own shortcomings. He knows that the mentor will analyse his business and his management abilities. That is as it should be and the mentoree recognises the need for it. On the other hand, it is more difficult for the mentoree to assess the mentor's experience of business, his awareness of its complications and his knowledge of the many complex situations faced by small business. After all, the mentor is, generally, on the mentoree's business premises and can see what the mentoree is capable of, whereas the mentoree is faced with a completely unknown person.

We saw in *Chapter 2* that the mentor can relieve the mentoree's anxiety about these considerations if he starts by giving him a potted biography of his own career to date. The sensitive mentor appreciates that it takes a big personality to accept and then state that there are aspects of his management skills that need improvement.

The mentor will tell the mentoree that he appreciates the mentoree's achievements to date and any successes he has enjoyed. He tells the mentoree that he has passed the first test of business — survival — no mean feat in itself, whatever the economic situation.

Mentoree's Goals

As stated previously, the mentor should, at the start of the mentoring assignment, discuss the needs and goals of the mentoree. It is also important that the mentoree is made aware of the goals of the mentor for the assignment. These goals should be discussed also.

Presumably the mentoree will have articulated his reasons for taking on a mentor. These reasons, usually, can be converted easily into goals for the assignment. Eventually, there must be a congruence of the goals of the mentoree and the mentor; otherwise, the assignment will set off on a confused basis.

Throughout the mentoring process, the goals can be reviewed to test their current validity. Usually a mentor completes the assignment on the lines agreed with the mentoree. But it doesn't have to be that way. As the process is one of continuous change, either participant can suggest a change of direction or, indeed, mentor, if it seems to be advantageous for a particular aspect of the process. After all, the mentoring process is a journey of search. Change was anticipated without knowing the nature of the change and neither party need be embarrassed about such a consequence. Indeed, it could be one of the success features of the process.

The agreed goals should be:

- **Clearly stated** so that everyone involved in their accomplishment understands what they are to do.

- **Measurable** because, as has been said many times, "what gets measured gets done".

- **Realistic** in terms of the resources available and the time span set for their completion.

- **Time-planned**, with the measures to be applied on specified dates.

What the Mentoree Gains from a Mentor

The benefits derived by a mentoree from a mentoring assignment vary from enterprise to enterprise. The sought-after outcome may not be the one that eventually materialises. But there are so many advantages that can be gained, given the right attitude, that it is normally a beneficial experience.

Some of the benefits are listed below:

- The moment the mentoree is prepared to accept the need for mentoring, he grows personally and professionally. It behoves the mentor to respect his humility and respond with similar modesty.

- The mentoree will find his personal skills improved or, at least, will have a better awareness how and where they can be improved. His political awareness, in a business sense, will be heightened.

- There will be gains in a range of intangibles — clearer insights, more confidence, greater stamina and stronger fortitude in face of adversity.

- The mentoree will have more humility and patience when confronted with the presumed inadequacies of others. He will have greater acceptance of the strengths and weaknesses of the people he works with and will have learned how to maximise their potential for their mutual benefit.

- Ideally, the mentoree will have gained increased respect for other people's points of view. It is advisable that the mentor shows by his questions and comments a respect for the opinions of others, even when he himself does not agree with them. The quest for improvement embraces consideration of as many suggestions as can be investigated in the time available before a decision has to be made. The object will have been to open the mentoree's awareness of alternate views.

- The mentoree will have learned to be more adaptable to business realities and changing business realities, that not every commercial ambition is possible or, indeed, desirable. His ambitions will not have been stultified or made look ridiculous because of their magnitude, but put in perspective having regard to the resources available and the time-frame contemplated.

- The mentoree will have developed the ability to cope with events beyond his individual control. A greater sense of commercial realism will have been engendered. The result will be a better awareness of the art of the possible.

- He will have acquired a better balance in his personal and work life. The joy he has in work will be enhanced because it has been made more meaningful. His work will be seen in its proper role in the totality of living. There is no problem in being dedicated to one's occupation. What must be avoided is becoming a workaholic, which removes all sense of proportion.

- He will have developed a more humane approach towards people in their work environment, their aspirations and professional problems. He, in turn, may see the benefit of his employees having a mentor for their careers.

WHAT MENTOREES LOOK FOR IN A MENTOR

The expectations of a mentoree will vary according to the stage of development of his business. If it is a business start-up, the process will be different from one where the business has been in existence for some time.

The principal characteristics sought by a mentoree in a mentor are:

- Abilities

- Qualities

- Attitudes.

Abilities

- **Listening Skill.** The mentor must be a good listener. This attribute is the essential characteristic of a mentor.

- **Questioning.** The mentoree anticipates many questions from the mentor as he learns about the mentoree's business history and his experience in it. He will expect the mentor to form an opinion about his experience. He anticipates that the mentor will assess his capability to achieve reasonable goals that the mentor and he will discuss and agree.

- **Competence.** The mentoree expects competence from the mentor. But competence in what? Does he look for a specific technical skill or is it a simple subconscious expectation of an air of competence? Perhaps it is an anticipation of some superior, if undefined, trait or quality of excellence that the mentoree feels a mentor should possess. If that is the case, the mentor may have some difficulty in satisfying such an expectation. The mentoree should be made realise that the mentor is fallible. It must be made clear that he does not have all the answers, although he may know where the answers can be found.

- **Technical Skills.** The entrepreneur approaches the mentoring programme seeking a mentor with a view to the acquisition of skill or skills in some aspect of his business. Having obtained a mentor and discussed the perceived needs (and reached agreement with the mentor that they were, indeed, the required skills), the mentoree seeks the opportunity and capacity to practise the acquired skills. And, lastly, he now desires the discipline to apply the skill.

- **Sympathetic Understanding.** On the other hand, he knows that the mentor expects him to be capable and forthright enough to present the best picture of his current situation. The mentor will assess the mentoree's perception of the mentoring process and how it will help him in his commercial ambitions. The mentoree expects the mentor to have a sympathetic understanding of all of these factors and help him to adapt to change. The mentoree hopes that the mentor is able to review his understanding of the mentoree's situation with him, in a way that helps the mentoree to understand it better himself.

- **Guide.** The mentoree must not expect the mentor to be a teacher. Teaching is different from mentoring. It has distinct objectives. There are teachers in other associations, courses and circumstances. The mentoring assignment is one of mutual search and guidance. Once again, we come back to the concept of a journey embarked upon by two people.

- **Contacts.** The mentoree expects the mentor to know where information relevant to his business is available and, if appropriate, to be able to put him in contact with business colleagues who could be of assistance to him.

- **Analytical Ability.** The mentoree wishes the mentor to help to check the rightness of the mentoree's thinking when confronted with a management or process problem. Hopefully, he will not be of the opinion that the wisdom of the mentor is immediately transferable or is the main purpose of the relationship.

Qualities

- **Broad Perspective.** What is clear to the mentoree is that it is acceptable for him to expect the mentor to have the ability, in the course of discussion, to develop his awareness of other aspects of his business. This is not to mention the possibility of helping him to conceive a wider perspective in his approach to his business.

- **Varied Perspective.** The mentoree should not expect the mentor to view everything from his perspective. One of the objectives of mentoring is to hear another opinion. At the same time, he looks for a sympathetic hearing of his point of view.

- **Stimulating.** Another expectation that the mentoree may have is that the mentor will check the mentoree's knowledge, stimulate his foresight, and nourish his drive.

- **Time scale.** The mentoree may wonder about the proposed length of the process on which he is about to embark. The mentor has told him that the process is one of transition, which ends at or about a certain time. The time scale is dictated by the goals mutually set and the progress towards their achievement. The mentoree expects that the relationship and the process will change as the assignment progresses.

- **Approachable.** Naturally, the mentor should not be stand-offish. That would make communication very stilted. A quiet sense of humour will facilitate the mentoring process.

- **Loyalty.** The mentoree expects the mentor to become a loyal friend. Loyalty is fundamental to the process. A genuine friendship may develop eventually. One thing is clear: the mentoree must not seek someone to lean on. A mentoring assignment is neither a refuge from problem-solving, nor a dumping of liability, nor a flight from reality, nor an abdication of responsibility.

Attitudes

- **Respectful.** The mentoree expects to be respected. That is his right. If the mentor cannot give him that respect, for whatever reason, he should withdraw from the assignment. The mentoree has had a measure of achievement in his field — conceivably, more achievement than the mentor has had in some or all of his projects. It is appropriate that this be recognised. And the corresponding respect should be manifest.

- **Non-Critical.** The mentoree should feel secure in his own position as mentoree. This means that the mentor should not appear a threat to his self-respect. The mentoree can expect sensitivity from the mentor as the matters under consideration touch the mentoree, his criteria and approach to problems in a very personal way. As we have seen so often, the principles of trust, respect, loyalty, and friendship are raised in the mentor–mentoree relationship.

- **Forthright.** The mentoree expects the mentor to be straightforward in his approach and frank in speech, without being blunt.

- **Positive Attitude.** It is reasonable for the mentoree to expect the mentor to have a positive attitude towards the mentoree and his business aspirations. He can anticipate an empathetic discernment of his feelings about his business, the business frustrations he has experienced, and his aspirations for his business.

- **Supportive.** The mentoree will hope to be supported by the mentor in solving problems, in the drafting of his plans and the subsequent achievement of them. The support is not tangible, of course. It is moral support. But it is honest support that manifests itself in a sincere analysis of the reasons for following a particular course of action. There may be times when sympathy is more appropriate, for example when the mentoree does not hit his target on time or experiences failure in a task or project.

WHAT MENTORS LOOK FOR IN A MENTOREE

The mentoree should realise that mentors look for specific qualities or characteristics in a mentoree. Different mentors will place more emphasis on some rather than others. The following are the more usual expectations:

- Abilities

- Qualities

- Attitudes

- Ethics/Values.

Abilities

- **Potential.** It is reasonable for the mentor to look for potential in the mentoree. The nature of that capacity is clear. He must have the desire to develop his business and the capability to do so, and the discipline to achieve the defined goals, albeit with the help and encouragement of the mentor, and others, if required.

- **Intelligence.** The mentor expects the mentoree to be reasonably intelligent and be capable of basic reasoned argument. He cannot be of help to the business if the person directing it finds it difficult to grasp simple management concepts. Communication is at the heart of the relationship between mentor and mentoree.

- **People Skills.** A mentor is sometimes amazed at the level of success a mentoree has achieved without any obvious skill in interpersonal relationships. The question is then "How did he do it without what seems an essential skill in business?" After all, as the saying goes, "business is people", whether they are customers or employees. How can an entrepreneur achieve any measure of success without people skills? Yet it happens. Is it the product being sold that generates success? Is the location of the business the critical factor? Is it the character of the employees, or some of them, that draws customers to the enterprise? Is interaction with people essential in that enterprise? Is there significant unemployment in the area, and people are pleased to have a job, any job? It is a constant source of surprise that some entrepreneurs survive and even achieve a significant level of success without this, seemingly, essential skill. The mentor would do well to analyse such a phenomenon when he encounters it.

- **Leadership.** Generally, the mentoree has shown some leadership qualities in creating the business or in achieving the position of chief executive of the business. The mentor can look to these qualities and their development to progress the mentoring assignment. This will be manifest in the willingness and ability of the mentoree to follow through and accomplish the tasks that he has agreed are achievable and which it is resolved are necessary.

Qualities

- **Ambition.** Can the mentor assume that the mentoree is ambitious to develop or improve his business? If he cannot, what is the point of the assignment? Has the assignment been forced on the mentoree by a State agency, financial institution, or some other outside body? If either is the case, the assignment is very probably doomed and the mentor should question the sense of continuing it.

- **Self-Motivated.** It is difficult to know how the mentor should respond if it becomes clear that the mentoree looks to him to be a motivator — that is, he believes that the mentor will indicate the path to be taken by the business and how the mentoree should direct its course. The mentoree may expect the mentor to stimulate him into a course of action. It is not the function of the mentor to be a motivator, although, on occasion, that is the consequence of the mentoring assignment. Where this occurs, the mentor should shift that particular burden back on to the shoulders of the mentoree where it properly belongs.

- **Trustfulness.** The question of trust is pervasive. It is a theme that runs through all writing, discussion and operation of a mentoring programme. Just as the mentoree expects commitment and loyalty from the mentor so, also, the mentor expects the same from the mentoree. He expects commitment to follow through with what is agreed and loyalty to the underlying concept of the mentor programme. The mentoree trusts the mentor to respect the confidentiality of facts that he reveals to him. He trusts him to be sympathetic to his ambitions. He trusts him to act objectively in the interests of his business without any private agenda.

- **Compatibility.** It is obvious that mentor and mentoree should be compatible. The friendship that is to be engendered, if the assignment is to succeed, is dependent on it. It would be impossible to achieve a mutual understanding if both parties are not able to reach agreement on objectives and processes.

- **Sense of Equality/Fairness.** The mentoree does not expect to be dominated by the mentor nor the mentor by the mentoree. Such a relationship would be disastrous for both parties. The mentoree may anticipate a reasonably powerful mentor personality and may be pleased or disappointed with the reality. The mentor should not become concerned with that type of visualisation of his role or character. Eventually, the mentoree will come to terms with the actuality. The progress of the assignment will, hopefully, give whatever reassurance he requires.

- **Loyalty.** The mentor can expect the mentoree to be loyal to the organisation that both he and the mentoree are endeavouring to improve as a result of the mentor assignment. It may seem strange to mention this topic. But it is not unknown for some entrepreneurs to view their business solely as a means to provide cash to facilitate a certain lifestyle without any reference to creating and maintaining a stable business. Their interest and loyalty to the employees who help provide the wealth is skin-deep.

- **Sense of Realism.** The mentor counts on willingness in the mentoree to face the truth about his business and the resources available to it, the reality about themselves and their capacity to achieve their ambitions.

- **Politically Aware.** The mentoree should be politically aware; that is, he should know what is acceptable in the business and social environment in which the enterprise operates, and respect the mores of that society. It helps if he is "street-wise" to some extent. Once again, it is a question of fitting in with the culture of the industry.

Attitudes

- **Reputable.** The mentoree should have a good reputation in the industry in which he and his business functions. He should be known for his honest and fair dealing and have earned respect for whatever success he has enjoyed. Survival in any business is a form of achievement, however limited that may seem. So much the better if he has grown the business and now wishes to renew it with the assistance of a mentor.

- **Supportive and Enthusiastic.** The mentor expects the mentoree to be supportive of the mentoring assignment and to demonstrate that support by participating in the process with energy and enthusiasm.

- **Disciplined.** The discipline expected of a mentoree is similar to that demanded of the mentor. The mentoree should be punctual, carry out agreed assignments, be considerate in making demands, be time-efficient (remember, the mentor has other mentorees and other interests), and ought not to expect hands-on involvement in the business by the mentor.

Ethics/Values

- **Share Common Values.** It is valuable if mentor and mentoree share common values. The answers to simple questions, such as what the mentoree hopes to achieve in his business and on what terms, and what he believes his mission is or should be, should be intellectually and morally acceptable to the mentor. Their interpretation of the primary goals of the business should be congruent.

4

THE RELATIONSHIP BETWEEN MENTOR AND MENTOREE

In the last two chapters, we reviewed the role and the characteristics of a mentor and what he looked for in a mentoree. We also examined the characteristics of the mentoree and what he looked for in a mentor. Those considerations were preparatory to the first meeting of the mentor with the mentoree. Now the action must start. The mentor must engage or, if you prefer, connect with the mentoree. In this chapter, we bring the two roles and expectations face-to-face to see how they should interact.

THE MENTOR/MENTOREE RELATIONSHIP

A good relationship between the mentor and mentoree is crucial to the success of the mentoring process. The mentor is to become the mentoree's guide, philosopher and friend, and so, initially, it is up to the mentor to establish this form of interaction. The co-operation of the mentoree is, needless to say, essential.

Both participants are about to embark on a journey and, ideally, they will travel hopefully. The mentor's credibility will be tested and his reliability proved. The mentoree's ability and stamina will be exposed and the suitability of the matching of the mentor with the mentoree revealed.

The relative brevity of the mentoring assignment in the life of the business means that the journey rather than the destination will be the focus.

The relationship of the mentoree with the mentor differs in every case. Not all are unqualified successes. The failure of one mentoring relationship does not mean that the mentoree is an unsuitable subject for mentoring or that the mentor is unqualified to be one. The reason for the failure should be examined, and, if thought appropriate, another mentor should be appointed.

As the journey progresses, the relationship of the mentor and the mentoree will develop in terms of trust, compatibility and friendship. If the process is to be successful, each meeting should result in improvements in credibility, recognition of dependability, trust and compatibility. *Figure 4.1* illustrates the correlation between the number of meetings, the passage of time and the status of the relationship. It shows a straight trend line (which may not be as straight in practice).

Figure 4.1: The Progression of the Mentor/Mentoree Relationship

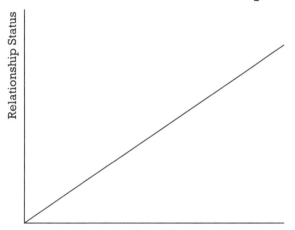

The development in their relationship will be reflected in the improved grades shown on the self-assessment charts (see *Figures 4.7*, *4.8*, *4.9*).

It is relevant at this juncture to bring together the various factors that will be the foundations of the mentoring process. The congruence of characteristics and expectations is set out in *Figure 4.2*.

Figure 4.2: Table of Congruence

Characteristics of a Mentor	What a Mentoree looks for in a Mentor	What a Mentor looks for in a Mentoree
Abilities	**Abilities**	**Abilities**
Listening Skills	Listening Skills	
Questioning	Guide by Questioning	
Technical and Mentoring Skill	Technical and Mentoring Skill	Potential & Intelligence
Ability to Empower	Guide	
Ability to Network	To have contacts	
Ability to Empathise	Sympathetic Understanding	People Skills
Analytical	Analytical ability	Leadership
Qualities	**Qualities**	**Qualities**
Experience	Broad and Varied Perspective	
Passion and Enthusiasm	Stimulation	Ambition & Self-Motivation
Timeliness	Timeliness	Commitment
Sense of Humour	Approachable	Compatibility
Capacity for Enjoyment		
Sense of Equality/Fairness		Sense of Equality/Fairness
Loyalty	Loyalty/friendship	Loyalty
		Sense of Realism
		Political Awareness
Attitudes	**Attitudes**	**Attitudes**
Respect for the mentoree	Respect for the mentoree	
Humility		
Willingness to take criticism	Non-critical	
Honesty	Forthright	Reputable
Caring	Positive	
Supportiveness	Supportive	Supportive and Enthusiastic
		Discipline
Ethics/Values	**Ethics/Values**	**Ethics/Values**
Ethical Conduct	Ethical Conduct	Share Common Values
Self-assessment		

Database of Mentoree Facts

The mentor prepares for his first meeting by compiling a database of known facts about the mentoree. Such obvious facts as name, address, telephone number, mobile phone number, fax number, e-mail and website addresses hardly need mention.

If immediately available, he should record type of industry, nature of business, product range, status in the industry, number of employees and regional or geographical spread of its market. He should obtain three years' financial reports. If these are not to hand, they should be obtained as soon as it is diplomatically appropriate.

Facts about the mentoree that are helpful in forging a good relationship should also be recorded. These include hobbies, likes and dislikes, and any personal details the mentoree chooses to volunteer. It may seem to be going too far to take a photograph of the mentoree but, in the career of a mentor, it may be difficult to recall every mentoree's face.

The First Mentor/Mentoree Meeting

In *Chapter 5*, there is a suggested agenda for and a reconstruction of a first meeting. *Figure 4.3* illustrates the first meeting process. As can be seen, it is a continuous process.

The Meeting and Sharing Process

Time spent talking about the business, its history and potential gives both parties the opportunity to evaluate one another. The mentoree wants to assess the mentor in respect of his ability to listen, preparedness to learn about the mentoree's industry and position of his business in it, empathy, communication skills and the relevance of the mentor's experience.

The mentor appraises the mentoree's perception of his business needs to see if they seem reasonable. And he wants to evaluate the personality of the mentoree to see whether they are likely to achieve rapport.

Personal openness between the mentor and mentoree is the best basis for an effective mentor process. The mentor promotes frankness by giving the mentoree a brief résumé of his career and experience to date.

Figure 4.3: The First Mentor/Mentoree Meeting

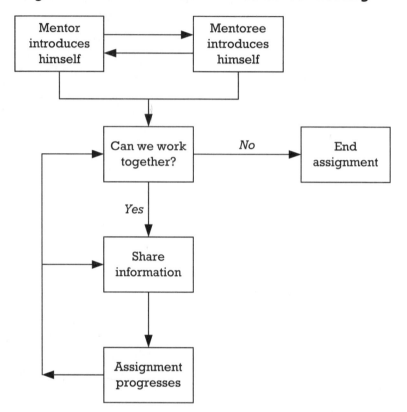

The mentor should explain to the mentoree that the flow of information will be two-way. He will tell him that some of the experience he will share with the mentoree has been gained from previous mentor assignments. And he will say that he expects to share the benefits of this assignment with other mentorees in the future (without divulging the identity or details of the current assignment).

The question both the mentor and mentoree must then answer is "Can we work together effectively?" If neither can say "Yes", the process is doomed to failure and should be ended forthwith.

The following points are important:

- How often have we been told that the customer is king? In the mentoring process, the mentoree is the customer. In that capacity, he is king. However, although the mentoree makes the decisions, both participants must agree the direction of the assignment.

- Experienced mentors believe that the most important function of the mentor is to ask questions. "Have you thought of?" and "What if?" questions encourage discussion about a proposed action or decision not to act.

- How many aspects of a proposed decision are there to consider? They can be countless, but paralysis by analysis is a risk. List the most important ones, and guide the mentoree by questions towards a decision. He decides.

- It is vital that mentor and mentoree have the same understanding of any problem or process that they are examining.

- The mentoree is likely to have an aspiration for his business and the mentor does not try to change it.

- Social compatibility is important but too much can be made of this aspect. It is sufficient if both can work together in a positive manner. The **Code of Conduct** for mentors (see **Appendix**) provides an excellent platform from which to develop a friendship on a proper basis.

- The mentor should give the mentoree a copy of his notes at the end of each meeting. The notes provide the mentoree with a record of progress to date and a list of things that he has decided to do.

- The frequency with which progress of the assignment is assessed will vary from business to business, but it is advisable to set dates for doing so at the outset.

- Progress is measured by comparing the extent of achievement to date with the ultimate goals agreed at the beginning.

- The assessments are not examinations or tests of either the mentor or mentoree. They are practical reviews that take into account the time spent and the time remaining.

Figure 4.4: The Meeting and Sharing Process

The mentor listens	→	**MEETING AND SHARING PROCESS**	←	The mentoree informs
The mentor questions	→		←	The mentoree clarifies
The mentor summarises	→		←	The mentoree listens
The mentor seeks options	→		←	The mentoree lists options
The mentor seeks goals	→		←	The mentoree selects goals
The mentor asks for priorities	→		←	The mentoree prioritises

The mentoree decides

Agreement between the Mentor and the Mentoree

When we say that there should be agreement between the mentor and the mentoree, we are conscious always that it is the mentoree who decides. The mentor can only test the mentoree's decision by asking questions. Therefore, by "agreement", we mean that the mentor believes that the mentoree's decision is likely to provide the most beneficial result.

If, on the other hand, the mentoree decides on a course of action about which the mentor has serious reservations, there is nothing the mentor can do other than ask questions that would indicate reservations. The questions will be of this nature:

- Are you satisfied that that is the best course of action?

- Are you quite sure that is the best thing to do?

- Should you take more time to consider what to do?

- Have you taken into account all the possibilities?

- Will that yield the optimum result?

If, in the mentor's opinion, the mentoree's decision is likely to bring disaster to the firm, should he resign? We think not. That implies that the mentor has a management function. However, if the mentor has reservations about a large number of decisions by the mentoree, it would suggest that there are irreconcilable differences of approach to business. In that circumstance, the mentor may have little to offer and should resign.

Agreed Objectives of Mentor Assignment

The discussion about the objectives of the assignment will take time. As stated earlier, that time is well spent. What is being discussed, at this meeting, will have a major impact on the outcome of the assignment.

Targets set by the mentoree, initially, can now be analysed in much more detail, to test their practicality in terms of resources available and time set for their achievement. If the objectives appear reasonable, but the time set for their completion does not seem realistic, should they be scaled back, or more time sought for the assignment?

The mentor does not set objectives for the assignment, nor does he approve objectives set by the mentoree. The targets set should be agreed. In any and every case, the mentor must ask himself, does the mentoree have the resources, including his own current level of skills and business awareness, to carry through a business plan?

In many assignments, the mentoree requires a mentor to help solve a particular functional problem in, say, production, sales or administration. There may be an exchange of technical information followed by discussion. The mentor must take care, however, not to assume the role of the mentoree. In all cases, the mentoree makes the decisions.

The mentor faces a problem if he is convinced that an objective proposed by the mentoree borders on the irrational. Applying his role as guide, philosopher and friend, he will keep asking questions about the target suggested until the mentoree either persuades him of its practicality, or convinces himself that it is unachievable (in the short term, at least). The mentor is not on the management team — the mentoree decides.

Goals

When there is agreement about the goals, they should be prioritised by the mentoree. It is obvious that agreeing and prioritising the goals is not sufficient. Action has to be taken to achieve the agreed objectives. *Figure 4.5* illustrates the simplest progression.

Figure 4.5: From Goals to Results

As stated previously, however, the goals must be quantified and be realistic within the timeframe envisaged. And so it may be necessary for the mentor to guide the mentoree through a process of rationalisation, as shown in *Figure 4.6*.

Furthermore, in some cases, the definition of goals and their timeframe is not adequate. The mentoring process may not last long enough for the mentor to see the achievement of the agreed goals within the time allotted. The timeframe envisaged may extend beyond the mentoring period. In such cases, interim goals should be defined, quantified, dated and pursued in the context of the ultimate goals.

Figure 4.6: From Goals to Results — The Detail

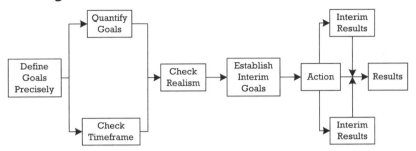

COMMUNICATION

The objective of any form of communication is to transfer information in a form that is understood by the recipient in the manner that is intended by the sender. Clarity in communication is not easy. Some of the major failures in communication arise from confusion between fact, opinion, and recommendation.

The mentor is not immune from this problem. If, in his career, no significant difficulties arose because of an occasional misunderstanding, he may not realise that lack of clarity could be a serious danger in a mentoring assignment.

As the function of the mentor is to be guide, philosopher and friend to the mentoree, any misunderstandings at the commencement or during the course of an assignment could undermine the mentoree's confidence in the process.

Perhaps the simplest way to avoid lack of clarity in communication with the mentoree is to form the practice of mentally distinguishing between fact, opinion, and recommendation before making a statement. Fact is the easiest to identify because the mentor is able to provide, or direct the mentoree to, supporting evidence. The real danger lies in causing confusion between opinion and recommendation. If the mentoree confuses an opinion with a recommendation and acts accordingly, there could be undesired consequences.

A mentor's opinion is usually expressed to provoke discussion or encourage the mentoree to consider it as one possibility. It will be followed by a debate between the mentor and mentoree. It is always made clear, however, that the mentoree makes the decision.

The Listening Mentoree

In *Chapter 1*, we emphasised the primary function of a mentor was to listen. We said "the mentor listens — and then speaks". It follows that when the mentor speaks, the mentoree, ideally, should then listen and comprehend. There is an essential difference between the mentor's approach and the mentoree's, however. The mentor can and should practise the art of listening. But he cannot *make* the mentoree listen. It follows that he must note whether the mentoree is paying attention to what he is saying, and, if he is not, use techniques to bring back his attention.

Some of the techniques are:

- **Stop Talking.** Paradoxically, an interval of silence can have more impact than continuous speech, music or noise. Orators and composers, through the ages, have made effective use of silences. The distracted mentoree will note the silence and curiosity, if nothing else, will make him attentive again.

- **Ask a question.** If the mentor suspects that the mentoree has lapsed into passive listening he will ask a question, not for information, but to return the mentoree to active listening. The mentor should be careful to introduce the question by saying, for example, "I should like to ask you a question. I mentioned xy and its effect on z process. Do you think that ... ?"

- **Make a Movement.** The movement should not be extreme, otherwise it could alarm the mentoree. It might simply be putting the notes on a table or desk, or excusing oneself before stretching one's legs by walking around the room, or removing or donning a jacket.

- **Demonstrate a Graph or Table of Figures.** Drawing a graph or compiling a small sample table of figures and requesting the mentoree to look at and consider their implication.

- **Invite Comment.** Ask the mentoree for his views on the subject under discussion. If necessary, give a résumé before he comments, thereby avoiding embarrassment.

- **Promote Group Discussion.** If there are several people at the mentor meeting and some are inattentive, suggest that there should be a discussion.

- **Introduce an Extraneous Topic.** This is a technique used by the managers of baseball teams. When a pitcher is not pitching well, the manager will walk on to the playing field and talk to him about something unconnected with the task on hand, for example, "I read in the paper today about a new sports car coming on the market . . ."

When the mentor speaks, it is important that the language used is appropriate to the audience. As a general rule, simple language is always suitable.

TRUST

It takes time to build trust between a mentor and mentoree. To trust a person, one must believe in their integrity, ability and character: a feeling that they will not fail in performance. Probably, the trust engendered in a mentoring process will never be a complete trust, because of the relatively short period of the assignment.

The mentor, for his part, should not be naïve. Testing buoys up trust. The mentor should be observant, although not motivated by suspicion, unless there may be good reason to be suspicious. It is advisable for him to be sensitive to "straws in the wind" and alive to innuendo, though he should take care not always to believe all he hears or reads.

How a mentor builds trust with a mentoree

The development of the mentoree's trust in the mentor derives from his perception of the mentor's credibility and reliability.

Credibility

The development of credibility begins with the first meeting of the mentor and mentoree. In a relaxed and friendly manner, the mentor tells the mentoree about his career to date, his experience and qualifications, thus outlining what he brings to the process.

If the mentor has been able to acquire the information we suggested for inclusion in his database (facts about the mentoree's industry and business, and about the mentoree himself), these can be referred to with caution in the course of the meeting.

By listening attentively to what the mentoree has to say, the mentor will show his respect for the mentoree and for his achievements to date.

The mentoree must be satisfied that the mentor has a clear understanding of what he wants the process to achieve.

Truthfulness at all times is essential to establishing credibility. It is no disgrace for the mentor to admit that he does not know the answer to a question. The mentoree must accept that the mentor is not omniscient.

The mentoree trusts the mentor to treat all information given to him as confidential. It is advisable for the mentor not to even mention the name of any mentoree to third parties. Some mentorees are curious about other mentorees who have been mentored by their mentor. Not saying who they were will underline to the mentoree the confidentiality of the process.

The mentor's commitment to the process must be unambiguous and made obvious to the mentoree.

The mentoree believes that the mentor will act in his best interest. What is in the mentoree's best interest is a matter of judgement, and is the mentoree's decision. If the difference of opinion is significant, the mentor can withdraw from the process. Nonetheless, it must be clearly seen that the mentor does not have a personal agenda.

The mentoree expects that the mentor will stay within his or her experience and expertise.

The mentor must never have a conflict of interest in anything with which the mentoree is involved. This applies, also, to any transactions in which a person with whom the mentor has a business or personal relationship is involved.

Reliability

It is most important for the mentor to be dependable. If he promises to do something, he should do it willingly and on time. This applies, for example, to such matters as sending a magazine article, looking up a reference.

Any action taken by the mentor should be undertaken in a manner that takes cognisance of the mentoree's preferred methods and customs.

Modes of speech, style of dress, general manner of communication that are appropriate to the character of the mentoree's firm are also important in impressing the mentoree with the mentor's reliability.

Consistency in performance and practices creates confidence and helps to engender trust.

How a mentoree builds trust with a mentor

The mentor expects the mentoree to tell the truth about the business, its history, its present position, and the mentoree's ambitions for the business. The mentor relies on the mentoree's integrity not to make a fool of him, by declaring statements of fact that are, in reality, wishes.

The mentor should feel confident that the mentoree will be loyal to him and the process and not let him down when tasks are to be performed.

The mentor expects the mentoree to conduct his business within the law and not to seek guidance in any illegality.

The mentoree should tell the mentor if, in his view, the mentoring process is living up to his expectations. It is advisable that the mentor encourages the mentoree to be frank about his assessment of the mentoring experience.

The mentor expects that all relevant facts about the business will be disclosed to him. This information may refer to other people and, indeed, there may be personal matters touched on.

MENTOR AS FRIEND

The idea of the mentor as friend of the mentoree was initially mentioned in *Chapter 2*. A friend is someone you like and trust and your trust and support is predicated on mutual openness and honesty in the relationship, and compliance with social and legal norms.

But friendship is multifaceted. There are many types of friendship with which we are all familiar. As in the case of trust between the mentor and mentoree, the friendship between mentor and mentoree takes time to establish and, is, of course, limited. And we do not forget that "Good fences make good neighbours".[8]

It is relevant, we believe, to consider the form of friendship that should exist between the mentor and the mentoree, because it will influence their interaction. The ease with which they communicate with one another will be a determining factor in the success, or otherwise, of the assignment.

It has been suggested that the mentor and mentoree are more like business comrades than business acquaintances, because they are associated in the advancement of a common cause or are engaged in struggling with a problem.

It is likely that the mentor and mentoree start as business acquaintances, advance to being business comrades, as described above, and, with the progress of the assignment, become "friends".

Clearly, as a general experience, a mentoree is not a close friend and would not be treated like family. There may be occasions where a mentor and mentoree develop a close friendship. But that does not happen often. It is not an objective of mentoring. They will always maintain their distinctive roles of mentor and mentoree.

ETHICAL CONSIDERATIONS

The relationship between the mentor and mentoree is a reasonably complex one. It is limited, as described above, to the mentoring assignment and the processes arising therefrom.

The mentor must not accept any appointment from the mentoree, such as a directorship or consultancy appointment or accept an invitation to invest in the company.

The mentor should not accept any gifts or hospitality, which could be interpreted as a form of bribery or corruption.

---

[8] Robert Frost, *Mending Wall (North of Boston)*.

The mentor should not write, sign or join in any recommendations of the mentoree's enterprise or products.

It is essential that the mentoree does not become emotionally dependent on the mentor.

The mentor must not get involved in any disputes between the mentoree and members of the mentoree's staff, or pursue a personal relationship of an emotional or sexual nature with a mentoree or a mentoree's employees.

The mentor must ensure that he does not drift into the management sphere or permit the mentoree to induce him to make management decisions.

MENTOR SELF-ASSESSMENTS

Although the mentoring assignment will be assessed formally at the conclusion of the process (**Chapter 9**), it is advisable for the mentor to conduct periodic self-assessments of the progress of the assignment during its currency.

The self-assessments should be made at reasonable intervals during the assignment, probably after the first, fourth, and seventh meetings, although some mentors may prefer to make the self-assessments after every meeting.

The objective of the self-assessment (see **Figures 4.7**, **4.8** and **4.9**) is to gauge how the mentor rates the progress of the process and what action he should take to improve his methods and correct any self-perceived shortcomings.

The column headed "Action for Improvement" provides space for the mentor to note what steps he should take to raise the level of achievement of the assignment.

As the assignment progresses the percentage of Total Points Scored to Total of Points Possible should increase. If not, a reappraisal of the process is essential, paying particular attention to the recorded "Action for Improvement" to see whether anything has been overlooked.

Figure 4.7: Mentor Self-Assessment

No	Question	1	2	3	4	5	6	7	8	9	10	Action for Improvement
1	Do I understand the industry?											
2	Do I understand the business?											
3	Am I clear about the goals/needs?											
4	Do I listen enough?											
5	Does the mentoree listen?											
6	Do I guide with questions?											
7	Is progress being made?											
8	Are meetings frequent enough?											
9	What is our relationship status?											
10	Does the mentoree make the decisions?											

Points Scored										
Total Points Scored										
Total Points Possible	100									
%										

Mark 1 to 10 (ten being the highest) by placing the letter X in the chosen box.

Calculate the points scored by totting the number of Xs in each column and multiplying by the appropriate number at the top of the column. Enter the totals in the relevant boxes in the row titled "Points Scored".

Cross-tot the figures opposite the heading "Points Scored" and enter opposite "Total Points Scored".

The Total Points Possible amounts to 100 — i.e. 10 questions × maximum of ten points each.

Express Total Points Scored as a percentage of the Total Points Possible and enter opposite the % sign.

Figure 4.8 is an example of a completed self-assessment after one visit:

Figure 4.8: Mentor Self-Assessment After One Visit

No	Question	1	2	3	4	5	6	7	8	9	10	Action for Improvement
1	Do I understand the industry?						X					More study required
2	Do I understand the business?					X						Ditto
3	Am I clear about the goals/needs?				X							Still under discussion
4	Do I listen enough?								X			Room for improvement
5	Does the mentoree listen?				X							Too soon to say
6	Do I guide with questions?							X				More care needed
7	Is progress being made?			X								Not relevant at this time
8	Are meetings frequent enough?			X								Ditto
9	What is our relationship status?		X									Continue as begun
10	Does the mentoree make the decisions?										X	

Points Scored		2	6	8	5	6	7	8	10
Total Points Scored	52								
Total Points Possible	100								
%	52								

The scores awarded reflect the early stage of the assignment. The lowest score refers to the mentor/mentoree relationship. After one meeting, it would not be credible to believe that a mature mutual trust had been established. The highest score underlines the reality that the mentoree makes all decisions. A lower mark would flag a major problem. It is not sensible to give a high mark to the progress of the assignment after the first meeting, despite any favourable impressions.

It is to be expected that the scores will improve as the process progresses. *Figure 4.9* is an example of a completed self-assessment after seven visits.

Figure 4.9: Mentor Self-Assessment After Seven Visits

No	Question	1	2	3	4	5	6	7	8	9	10	Action for Improvement
1	Do I understand the industry?								X			Read more industry mags
2	Do I understand the business?										X	
3	Am I clear about the goals/needs?										X	
4	Do I listen enough?									X		Eternal vigilance
5	Does the mentoree listen?						X					Use more techniques
6	Do I guide with questions?										X	
7	Is progress being made?										X	
8	Are meetings frequent enough?							X				Shorten intervals
9	What is our relationship status?										X	
10	Does the mentoree make the decisions?										X	

Points Scored						6	7	8	9	60
Total Points Scored	90
Total Points Possible	100
%	90

In this case, the scores show a significant improvement, as one would expect. The score for the mentor/mentoree relationship is at the optimum. The mentoree still makes all the decisions! The action for improvement column indicates areas where much work still has to be done.

CONCLUSION

If the definition of mentor as guide, philosopher and friend is to be taken seriously, it seems logical that an appreciation of its significance is part of the mentor's preparation.

The mentor as guide indicates the way or manner in which problems and processes should be addressed.

Mentoring assignments have a beginning, a process, and an end. If, during the course of a mentoring assignment, a mentor believes that the assignment has come to a point where another mentor's skill would be more beneficial to the mentoree, he should recommend to the mentoree a change of mentor. Or, if the need is in a specialist activity, he may recommend the addition of another mentor.

There is a time to terminate an assignment, and not just when it has run its course. This may be at a point where it is obvious to the mentor that the mentoree is well capable of continuing without the attendance of the mentor or where the mentoree is not taking advantage of the help being made available to him.

Mentoring is an art that requires constant renewal. The mentor refreshes his skill by keeping up-to-date in management thinking, management practices and developments in the means of communication. At the mentoring meetings, the mentor's training, knowledge, and experience is made available to the mentoree to reinforce his business acumen, information, and experience. The mentor's knowledge should be up-to-date.

Objectivity is expected from a mentor in his communication with a mentoree. He will be detached but not disinterested. Most important of all, he will *listen* to the mentoree.

It is music to a mentor's ears when, at the end of an assignment, the mentoree says, "Thank you for the benefit of your experience."

5

THE FIRST MEETING

The purpose of the first meeting is to introduce the mentor and mentoree to one another, establish rapport, agree the objective(s) of the mentoring assignment and familiarise the mentor with the mentoree's business.

This chapter should be read in conjunction with **Figure 5.1**.

Figure 5.1: Agenda for the First Meeting

Introduction to Mentoring	The mentor explains to the mentoree the way in which the mentoring assignment is to be progressed.
Objective of Mentoring Assignment	The mentoree tells the mentor what he hopes to achieve as a result of the mentoring assignment.
Introducing the Mentor	The mentor tells the mentoree about himself, his qualifications, his career to date, his special interests, and, if possible, how he will approach the assignment.
Introducing the Mentoree	The mentoree tells the mentor about himself, his business, products, markets, management structure, number of employees, premises and size of investment.
Inspection of the premises	The mentoree shows the mentor around the premises, explains the production processes and introduces key executives.
Research and Development	The mentoree tells the mentor about the R&D programme, if one exists, outlining its objectives.

Marketing	The mentoree tells the mentor about the firm's marketing programme, if one exists, outlining the personnel involved.
Selling	If there is a sales function separate from the marketing function, the mentoree will describe how this function operates.
Special Projects	The mentoree will list any once-off or periodic activities or operations such as relocation of storage, installation of a computer, annual audit, a special costing exercise for a sales programme or new product.
Personnel	The mentoree tells the mentor the number of employees and how they are deployed, the training policy of the company, if any, the quality improvement programme in operation, if any, any recruitment in progress. It would be relevant to ask about the company's use of outsourcing.
Premises	The mentoree tells the mentor what plans, if any, he has to develop the premises, move to new premises, or renovate the existing premises.
Equipment	The mentoree lists the equipment, new or used, which will be required for the expansion of the business. Major repairs outstanding will also be mentioned.
Finance	The mentoree tells the mentor what financial reports he is given each period, monthly, quarterly, or annually, from internal sources, or externally by the company's auditor.
Any Other Business	This provides an opportunity for the mentoree to talk about topics not specifically listed in the agenda, and for the mentor to raise matters that occur to him from the conversation up to this point.
Task for Next Meeting	Under this heading, the mentoree lists the task or tasks that he intends to complete before the next mentor meeting.
Date of Next Meeting	It is most important to agree the date of the next meeting.

The mentor enters the managing director's office, shakes hands with him and sits down. The mentor and the managing director, who is the mentoree, exchange a few pleasantries. Then:

Mentor: Tell me, why did you ask for a mentor?

Mentoree: It may have been a feeling of frustration, I suppose. The company is small but is developing OK, more or less, but the management seems to be caught up, increasingly, in dealing with day-to-day matters. We are getting new customers and new business, but there doesn't seem to be a sense of purpose. When we started this company, every day was exciting and challenging. Things happened. I suppose we made them happen. Now, there doesn't seem to be the same verve, the same feeling of action. I'd say we have lost our sense of direction and we need someone to help us take a fresh look at our business, at the company. I suppose you could say that we are like a ship without a rudder, or, with a damaged rudder, anyway. We don't have a business plan, for example, and the financial institutions seem to expect one. Our budgeting is fairly basic. I'm not sure that you would call it budgeting. An outsider, a third party, as it were, such as you, may be able to help us. You see, I don't have anyone in the business to talk to who knows about these things.

Mentor: Do you think that there is a need for fundamental change, or is it a case of making some improvement?

Mentoree: Change undoubtedly. How fundamental a change, I don't know. We are profitable. How long that will last is another question. We need to decide where the company is going.

Mentor: I can sympathise with your frustration. It happens in most businesses several times in their existence. It is a bit like pausing for breath. There are times when things seem worse than they are, and all that is needed is a relatively small change.

Mentoree: You may be right. Where do we go from here?

The mentor, having listened to the mentoree's initial thoughts, decides to explain to him the way in which the mentoring assignment is progressed.

Mentor: Do you know how the mentor system works?

Mentoree: Not really. No.

Mentor: Let me explain, briefly. And please don't hesitate to ask any questions which occur to you as I talk. Essentially, the mentor acts as a kind of sounding board for your ideas. We listen.

Mentoree: Does that mean that you won't make any suggestions?

Mentor: Not exactly. You have been managing this business for some time. You know a good deal more about it than I do. Also you probably know what you would like to do with the business. My task is, most likely, to give you the opportunity to air your views with a third party, and to help you to articulate your ambitions for the company. I will try to explore the options that are available to you. Then later, I will help you produce a plan for further development of the company.

Mentoree: How do you propose to do that?

Mentor: By asking questions. For example, the first question I usually ask is, "Do you feel that you are working *on* your business or *in* your business?"

Mentoree: I see. Sometimes I feel I am working *under* my business. But to be serious, do you just ask questions?

Mentor: In general, yes. Indeed, it has been unkindly suggested that it would be as effective if a cardboard cut-out of a mentor was sent to a mentoree, provided he promised to talk to it, about his business, of course, for a period of at least two hours every month. In other words, take time to view the business as a whole instead of dealing with immediate tasks or problems on a day-to-day basis.

Mentoree: I take your point. These mentor meetings, then, are intended to make sure that, on a regular basis, I actually think about my business from a different perspective. To work *on* my business rather than work *in* my business?

Mentor: Yes, that is the general idea. The goal of this mentor programme is to make available to proprietors of small and medium-sized enterprises (SMEs) someone who has many years' experience of business, preferably of several businesses. That is, someone who is prepared to share his or her knowledge with entrepreneurs who are going through phases of a business cycle of which the mentor has had experience. The mentor is someone who the businessman can talk to and who will, hopefully, become the entrepreneur's friend and discuss the business from that perspective. The entrepreneur, ideally, will benefit from talking to an experienced businessperson who will discuss his business, its plans, and any problems it may have.

Mentoree: How do you do that?

Mentor: To start with, the mentor's task is to listen to what the proprietor of an SME has to say about his business. If the entrepreneur perceives business challenges and/or problems, the mentor helps him to deal with them and to guide him in the development of his plan or plans for the expansion of his business.

Mentoree: Does that mean you will help me to draw up a business plan?

This is the second time that the mentoree has mentioned a business plan. The mentor wonders whether the mentoree has made the drafting of a business plan the objective of the mentoring assignment.

Mentor: Is your objective for these mentoring sessions the drafting of a business plan?

Mentoree: It is certainly one of my objectives. Others may emerge as we progress. I am sure that, as we work on the business plan, we will identify gaps in knowledge, poor systems, maybe even the absence of systems. But to get back to my original question, will you help me to draw up a business plan?

Mentor: Of course, but not by direct input and not hands-on, so to speak.

Mentoree: How do you mean?

Mentor: I believe that you and, indeed, most businesspeople, are able to prepare a plan in some form for their own business. It is possible that I may be able to guide you in the methodology of preparing a plan. I may be able to help you to develop the plan further by asking questions such as, for example, how one part of the plan might have an impact on another part. A goal stated in one part of the plan will usually require a list of actions to be taken in another part of the plan.

Mentoree: I'm not sure I follow you.

Mentor: I will give you an example. If you plan to increase your sales by 40 per cent over three years, specific actions must be taken to achieve that goal. The actions may include recruiting additional marketing and/or sales personnel, introducing new products, the preparation of sales promotions, more training for sales staff, to mention but a few.

Mentoree: I understand. That sounds good to me. How do we start?

The mentor now introduces himself in more detail with a view to establishing better rapport and demonstrating transparency and openness in the relationship.

Mentor: Usually it is helpful to start with you telling me about yourself, how you started your career and what made you decide to go into business in the first place, when the company was founded and how it developed to this point, and so on. But before you do that, you might like to know something about me?

Mentoree: Yes, I would like to know how you became a mentor.

Mentor: I am an accountant by training. After my apprenticeship, I spent 28 years in practice specialising in business start-ups but with a portfolio of audits as well. Some years ago, I decided I wanted a change, primarily to focus on business planning and financial controllership. I developed a small business in that area and, later, became involved in the mentor programme. During my apprenticeship I was fortunate enough to have a mentor. He wasn't called a mentor at the time, of course, but I realise now that that is what he was. Not only did he become a friend and my guide in many technical matters, he introduced me to several other topics not directly related to my profession. You could say that he was also my philosopher. And so here I am. That is a quick summary. No doubt, more details will emerge during our meetings. Any questions?

Mentoree: Have you been mentor to a company as small as this one?

Mentor: Yes, I have, and to smaller companies also. The variety is fascinating and instructive. I should say the mentor learns too from each business he visits. Each mentoring assignment adds to his experience, which he can then share with others.

The mentor would like to give the mentoree an opportunity to talk some more. As he stated, more details of the mentor's career will emerge as the assignment progresses.

Mentor: Now, I should like you to tell me something about you and your company.

Mentoree: My wife and I formed this company about ten years ago. Prior to that, I worked for a company that manufactured widgets. The company was in Germany. I gained a lot of experience there and I enjoyed working for them. However, my wife never settled and was homesick, so we packed our bags and returned to Ireland. For some time, before we left Germany, I had an idea that, whereas widgets were very effective in their application, another product, which I called twidgets, had the possibility of being at least as effective and could be produced more economically.

Mentor: Did you do any work on the twidgets in Germany?

Mentoree: No. It was just a concept at that time. I knew that it was chancy to think of starting a business with an untried product but I was young and, perhaps, foolish. My wife gave me her full support.

Mentor: Had you to do a lot of research?

Mentoree: Months and months. Most of it in the kitchen of our rented house in Ireland. Later, when I leased a small industrial unit, I produced a prototype, which was then tested rigorously by a product testing facility in one of the universities. It seemed to work to the potential I had visualised. My wife took a job at the time to help make ends meet.

Mentor: Still pretty risky?

Mentoree: Sure. But here we are. If you don't believe in yourself nothing will happen, because you will do nothing.

Mentor: You are absolutely right. I have worked with several people who started their businesses in sheds at the bottom of their garden and, after a few years, expanded into industrial units. So you are in the engineering industry?

Mentoree: You could say that. And we supply manufacturers mainly. Maybe, if you saw the product and the production lines you would have a better idea of what I am talking about. Afterwards, I will show you some of its uses.

Mentor: That is a good idea. But before we go, how many people do you employ?

Mentoree: Just ten.

Mentor: How are they divided?

Mentoree: I am the managing director, obviously. My wife looks after the accounts. I have a marketing person. She has been with us almost since the start. I learned a most important lesson in Germany: that a good product is valueless lying in a warehouse. It must be sold. We have just recruited an assistant for her. We have to see how that will work out. Then, there is the production supervisor and four operatives and one general jobber who packs and cleans up in the factory.

Mentor: I see you have a team and a management structure in place.

Mentoree: I hope so. Shall we go? I'll lead the way.

The managing director and the mentor go on to the factory floor. The mentor is introduced to the production supervisor. The mentor explains the purpose of the mentor programme to the production supervisor. The production supervisor then shows the mentor around the factory, demonstrates the product and explains the production process. The mentor notes that the packing section and the materials and finished product storage areas are untidy. He is also of the opinion that the production flow is not as efficient as it could be. As the mentor is not a production expert, although he has seen many production lines during his career, he makes a mental note to recommend a production mentor at a fu-

ture date. The mentor and the managing director return to the managing director's office.

Mentoree: What did you think?

Mentor: Very interesting and impressive. I can see that you have come a long way since your initial concept. There seems to be a very good relationship between the operatives on the production line and the supervisor. The tour of the production area gave me a good idea about the product too. At this first meeting I concentrate, usually, on familiarising myself with all aspects of the business. That means, I ask a lot of questions about the various departments, what they do and who manages them. I hope you don't mind if it seems to be a bit like an interrogation. It isn't intended to be and the questions are not intended to pressurise you in any way. Some of my questions, as you will see, may be irrelevant because of my lack of knowledge of your company. Some things I may appear to just touch on, but we will return to these at future meetings. So, do you mind if we start?

Mentoree: Not at all.

Mentor: Who designed the production layout?

Mentoree: I did.

Mentor: Did you have any help?

Mentoree: No. The layout is based on principles I read in a management magazine and which I have seen applied in Germany. I know that it is not perfect — but, we can only try.

Mentor: I was not being critical, but I have a few ideas, which may be helpful. If you like, we can talk about that another time.

The mentor is keen to know, at an early stage of the assignment, if the company is relying on its current product line or if it appreciates the need for continuous improvement in its products.

Mentor: Are you continuing to develop your twidgets product?

Mentoree: How do mean?

Mentor: Do you have a research and development programme?

Mentoree: We don't have one in any formal sense. But if we see — that is, the production supervisor and I — the need for a modification of the product, we modify it. Also sometimes, a customer makes a suggestion. We always look at those very carefully. Do you think that we should have a research and development programme?

Mentor: It is generally recommended to keep a company's products under constant review. As you know, no market stands still. New competitors enter the market with new and/or improved products and firms that have not upgraded their own products can be caught out and sustain significant loss of sales.

Mentoree: As you have seen, we are a small company and we do not have the resources to embark on a research and development programme.

Mentor: I'm not suggesting an expensive R&D programme. You have the skill. You developed the twidgets originally, with some help from the university's engineering department. Do you think that that successful programme should be continued?

Mentoree   Why?

Mentor: To keep your product ahead of the competition and make sure that your current success continues.

Mentoree: I don't know of any product that competes directly with ours.

Mentor: That can change, can't it?

Mentoree: I suppose so. Now that I think of it, there are some aspects of the product that could be refined, and, maybe, could provide us with a second product.

Mentor: Does that mean that you could regard the original product or its technology as a product platform?

Mentoree: Meaning?

Mentor: A product platform comprises subsystems and interfaces that are, or could be, common to several products. They provide the basic elements for developing related products. Your twidget on the other hand may derive from processes. Is it an assembled product?

Mentoree: To some extent. Yes, although we do manufacture several of the components ourselves.

Mentor: In that case, the platform takes in sourcing components, assembly and testing.

Mentoree: That is all very well, but there just doesn't seem to be the time to work on them.

Mentor: That is a problem we all have regularly. Planning often produces time by eliminating time wasted elsewhere on, perhaps, irrelevant activities. Delegation is another possibility. It seems to me that we should incorporate R&D into the development plan. Formalising the activity in this way keeps it in focus. It would be a pity not to apply the skill you have for product development.

Mentoree: If you think that that would help. I know it's true I should make more use of my flair for design.

Mentor: Other companies that I have worked with have found that an active R&D programme is essential. Many of them strove to advance up the technological ladder to reduce competition from "Fred in the Shed", and to make the cost of entry for others prohibitive. Let me draw you a diagram of what I call the "Progress Pyramid".

Figure 5.2: The Progress Pyramid

Mentor: As you can see, as each more advanced product is introduced, the market narrows as the numbers with such sophisticated needs and the resources to purchase it are reduced. At the same time, the rate of gross profit can be increased because at the more advanced technological level competition is less and generally the consumer is not as price conscious. Furthermore, the cost of acquiring the production resources, personnel and financial, also increases thereby making it more expensive for new competition to enter the market.

The mentor passes the paper to the mentoree who examines it for a few moments and then puts it to one side. The mentor moves on.

Mentor: What are the benefits of the product?

Mentoree: It's very strong, it's cheap, and it is a quality product.

Mentor: What are the benefits for the end-user, the consumer?

Mentoree: I don't know what you mean.

Mentor: Have you heard of the "Consumer's Prayer"?

Mentoree: I can't say I have.

Mentor: "Do not offer me things. Offer me ideas, emotions, ambience, feelings, benefits."

Mentoree: I remember now: "Do not offer me shoes. Offer me comfort for my feet and the pleasure of walking. Do not offer me a house. Offer me security, comfort, and a place that is clean and happy. Do not offer me books. Offer me hours of pleasure and the benefit of knowledge." And so it goes on.

Mentor: Exactly. Can you talk to me about your product in those terms, that highlight the benefits to the consumer and, hopefully, will make him want to buy it?

Mentoree: I certainly can do so, but not right now. It's a good idea and worth spending some time on it.

Mentor: Many companies make consumer benefits the core of their business plan.

Mentoree: Of course, that makes a lot of sense.

Mentor: Following on from that, how do you manage your marketing programme?

Mentoree: As I told you earlier, we have a marketing person and a new assistant marketing person. I was thinking that the new person would start by doing the more humdrum work previously done by the marketing person. This would free her up to get out of the office more and interact with the customers.

Mentor: I notice that you refer to her as a marketing person. Does she have a title, such as Marketing Manager?

Mentoree: I never gave her that title, although, I noticed that she signed some letters last week as Marketing Manager. That was something I was going to ask you about. Should I give her a title?

Mentor: I'm not in a position to say. At this time, I am just becoming familiar with your business and when, during future meetings, we discuss the business plan, matters like that will come up for your decision. In your marketing programme, what methodology is used?

Mentoree: I meet the marketing person weekly, last thing on Friday, and we review the sales for the past week and the year to date and compare the figures with those of last year. We then discuss and, yes, plan the activity for the following week. There are usually other matters discussed, such as travelling, maybe discounts or rebates some customers have asked for and so forth. Of course, if there are any problems with any customer we discuss that too.

Mentor: Would you say that those are "bread and butter" issues, in terms of marketing?

Mentoree: Very much so. But they have to be done.

Mentor: Indeed they do. Does the marketing person submit a report? Are the meetings formal?

Mentoree: Oh no, informal. You see, there are just the two of us. I haven't seen the need for a written report. Would it be helpful if the marketing person joined us?

Mentor: If you think so.

The marketing person comes into the office and exchanges greetings with the mentor. The mentor tells her about the mentoring programme and that he is acquainting himself with all aspects of the business. He mentions, also, that a marketing plan has been discussed. He stresses that he is not acting as a consultant and makes clear that he is a guide and friend.

Mentor: We were talking about the weekly marketing meetings you hold. Do you have an agenda? Do you keep minutes?

Marketing person: We never thought of doing so. Should we?

Mentor: Many successful business people I have met, who were deeply involved in the marketing function, think it is better to do so. Let me show you an agenda. It is, necessarily, generic. You will want to amend it for your own purposes but it may be of some help.

Figure 5.3: Agenda for Weekly Marketing Meeting

No.	Item	Action	Who	When
1.	Objectives of meeting			
2.	Minutes			
3.	Matters Arising			
4.	New Business 4.1 New Customers 4.2 Existing Customers 4.3 Probable 4.4 Quotations o/s			
5.	Marketing 5.1 Marketing Activities 5.2 Capture Programme 5.3 Customer Review 5.4 Customer Satisfaction 　　Questionnaire			
6.	New Products			
7.	Marketing Personnel 7.1 Number 7.2 Recruitment 7.3 Training 7.4 No. of suggestions 　　made 7.5 No. of suggestions 　　implemented			
8.	AOB			
9.	Achievements of meeting			
10.	Improvements for next meeting			
11.	Date of next meeting			

Mentor: Do you discuss the coming week in any detail? Do you quantify the planned activities?

Mentoree: We discuss what will be done the following week, as I said. Can you be more specific?

Mentor: Some well-known marketing directors recommend quantifying the marketing activities. For example, if you plan to send some direct mail, isn't it better to decide how many letters will be mailed? If you plan to make phone calls to make appointments, isn't it helpful to know how many you intend to make?

Marketing person: Possibly. What then?

Mentor: Would it be useful to know how many letters were actually sent, how many phone calls were actually made, how many appointments were made? And give reasons for any significant variance?

Mentoree: And this would be useful in what way?

Mentor: You would then have an exact record of the extent of a marketing activity and be able to evaluate it when reviewing sales achieved?

Mentoree: Or not achieved!

Mentor: Exactly.

Marketing person: We haven't done that so far. We discuss the activities but the activities are not quantified.

Mentoree: Presumably quantification of activities will be incorporated into our marketing plan.

Mentor: Many companies do so. It forms part of the supporting information for the marketing budget. You could say that it provides the critical linkage between activities and results. Do you have a marketing budget?

Mentoree: I have a good idea what we will spend but here again we could probably be more specific for control purposes. I suppose you would expect us to go into the budgeting aspect in more detail. We have an overall budget for the next year. It is not very detailed.

Mentor: At the beginning, you said that your objective for this mentoring assignment was to get guidance in the preparation of a business plan. We will need to talk about the overall budget in detail during the next few meetings. In the meantime, after we have discussed the core capability of the company and the company's mission, within the parameters set thereby, the marketing plan is the first part of the business plan to be tackled.

Mentoree: We haven't really gone into that aspect at all. The lack of precision in this area is, I suppose, a fair reflection of the general lack of focus that I spoke to you about earlier.

Marketing person: It's all very well to draw up a marketing plan but we are dependent on what the market decides.

Mentor: That is true. Very few marketing plans survive intact when confronted by hostile market forces. But a plan gives a sense of direction.

Marketing person: I agree.

Mentor: Do you distinguish between marketing and selling?

Marketing person: We don't really make a distinction. I remember hearing at a marketing course that marketing created the desire to buy and that selling was making the sale.

Mentor: Do you see any advantage in making such a distinction in practice?

Marketing person: Perhaps, although I wonder if it would have any meaning in a company of our size.

Mentoree: At the same time, I'm beginning to see the general direction you are going in. To plan, we will break down every activity into its constituent parts and quantify activities under each heading.

Mentor: And then?

Mentoree: And then what?

Mentor: And then express the activities in cash terms.

Mentoree: For inclusion in the business plan.

Mentor: Exactly. Do you anticipate any difficulty in doing that?

Mentoree: Time. Only time. But I suppose we will have to find the time.

Mentor: It is worth spending the time on planning. In due course, it makes the enterprise more efficient because things get done and on time, it reduces costs and, indeed, saves time. It acts as a discipline, which helps you make sure that skills are applied in their proper area. Also, it enables flexibility of response to variances from the plan because the net result of deviations from the plan can be assessed and appropriate remedies applied.

Mentoree: I can see the benefits.

Mentor: Now I would like to move on to other topics.

Mentoree: Can we excuse the marketing person?

Mentor: Of course.

The mentor thanks the marketing person for her help and she leaves the mentoree's office.

Mentor: Do you have any special projects that are ongoing?

Mentoree: Such as?

Mentor: Installation of a new filing system, introducing a new costing system, drafting a company manual, changing the location or layout of raw materials, the annual audit . . . any once-off project activity which occurs infrequently.

Mentoree: Not that I can think of off-hand. Why do you ask?

Mentor: One company, to which I was mentor, found it useful to classify any such activity as a special project and monitor it separately from the day-to-day activities. Special Projects was a separate heading on their agenda. Once a particular task was completed, it was removed from the agenda.

Mentoree: We seem to be working towards agenda-driven meetings.

Mentor: A lot of business people find it beneficial to do so.

Although the mentoree had outlined the staffing of the company at the beginning of the meeting, the mentor may wish to discuss it at more length.

Mentor: Earlier, you gave me a general overview of the company's employees. Would you mind telling me again the number of employees you have, including yourself?

Mentoree: Ten.

Mentor: Are they unionised?

Mentoree: No.

Mentor: How do you negotiate salaries and wages?

Mentoree: I deal with the marketing person, the production supervisor and the general handyman individually. The operatives have appointed a spokesperson, who negotiates with me.

Mentor: When do you have these discussions?

Mentoree: Each year when the audited accounts are available. Actually, I have just finished this year's negotiations.

Mentor: I know that you have told me before, but to refresh my memory, the employees are divided into which departments?

Mentoree: I am the managing director. My wife looks after the accounts and the administration. When we were in Germany, she studied bookkeeping at night school. She attended a week-long course on computers too. There are two people in marketing, as I said previously. Then there is the production supervisor. He is a very good man, very conscientious. There are four operatives and the general handyman.

Mentor: That number of people requires a good deal of management. Do you have a staff training programme?

Mentoree: Training is ongoing in an *ad hoc* sort of way. New staff are trained on the job they are expected to do. From to time, they are shown how to improve performance. Occasionally, the supervisor goes to a course or seminar on some aspect of supervision or staff relations. And, of course, the marketing person attends an occasional seminar. I am not sure if that answers your question.

Mentor: The training given to new staff, is that part of an induction programme?

Mentoree: Can you expand on that question?

Mentor: Do you have an induction manual that welcomes new employees to the company and introduces them to its mission, its products, its organisation, its personnel, and house rules, such as working hours and so forth?

Mentoree: As I said, training is very much, let's say, unplanned. I say unplanned, because you seem to be concentrating on the extent to which our activities are planned. I don't have a problem with that, because that is one of the reasons I asked for a mentor.

Mentor: Is there a figure for staff training in your budget?

Mentoree: As I already said, I never thought about staff training in a formal way. I should like to think about having an induction manual. From what you said, it could help us to remember all the things we should say to new recruits. Presumably we will be discussing the contents of such a manual at some time in the future.

Mentor: Yes, if you would like to.

Mentoree: The idea of a training programme, is that just a list of courses? Are you sure that it is not another way of spending hard-earned money with no benefit to the company?

Mentor: Not if it is planned to benefit the company and add to its bottom line. In answer to your first question, not entirely. Companies develop a training policy related to the objectives set out in the business plan. Then they decide on the training objectives and how to achieve those objectives. It goes without saying that these training objectives are linked to the achievement of the other objectives of the business plan. A person is appointed to manage the training programme. From there, the training budget is calculated, which in turn will be included in the company budget.

Mentoree: It seems to follow the planning pattern of other activities in the business.

Mentor: Exactly, and it is integrated with the objectives of the overall plan. And training is a basic element in creating employee enthusiasm. Allied to that, in a way, have you considered a quality programme or business excellence programme?

Mentoree: Here again, we have discussed something similar, related to customer service. I have read about those programmes, of course, but so far they have been noted only as yet another activity that we would like to become involved in down the road.

Mentor: You have, obviously, thought about the subject — customer awareness in all its aspects, customer care, customer satisfaction, all aspects of the business focused on the customer.

Mentoree: Indeed. I dare say that that is something that we should be emphasising all the time.

Mentor: Are you recruiting any additional staff at present?

Mentoree: No. But, from this conversation, it looks as if I will be.

Mentor: Why do you say that?

Mentoree: I was joking.

Mentor: Many a true word is spoken in jest. It may not be possible to do everything we are discussing at present. In due time, when we consider all the business aspects under consideration, some will be given more prominence than others. It will be necessary to prioritise. And, as it is said, "Cash is king." You must have cash to do these things. Do you anticipate having to recruit staff within the next two to three years?

Mentoree: I think so. Logically, if the company expands, I will have to.

Mentor: In which departments?

Mentoree: Production.

Mentor: What about marketing?

Mentoree: I hadn't thought about them in that context. If we separate marketing from selling, perhaps, the recruitment should be for a pure sales person.

Mentor: What percentage of total overhead expenditure is spent on marketing?

Mentoree: I don't know.

Mentor: Is it greater or lesser than that on administration?

Mentoree: Possibly more is spent on administration.

Mentor: Do you think that is appropriate for a business?

Mentoree: I don't know.

Mentor: When I asked another entrepreneur that question, he replied that he wasn't running an administration service. To him, everything in the business revolved around the marketing function. All other activities, including production, were service functions — that is, servicing the marketing department.

Mentoree: I hadn't thought of this business in that way. Usually, finance is regarded as the most important

function in any business but you have given me a
different perspective.

Mentor: It was. But there have been changes in management thinking. When finance was dethroned as the
centre of the business activity universe, it was re-
placed by marketing. Subsequently, marketing
was expected to share centre stage, as it were,
with research and development. You could illustrate it this way.

The mentor takes a sheet of paper and draws.

Figure 5.4: The Business Activity Universe

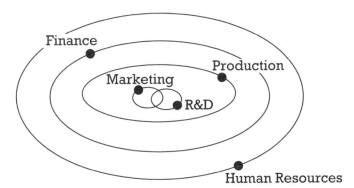

*The mentor passes the paper to the mentoree who looks at it for a
moment and smiles before putting it beside the other diagram.*

Mentoree: A picture is better than a thousand words. It does
throw a fresh light on the structure of a business
organisation. How to implement it is another thing,
but that is what we are here to do, isn't it?

Mentor: Absolutely.

Mentoree: All this suggests more employees. And more employees mean more work for me.

Mentor: Not if you delegate. Do you think that you have the
confidence to delegate?

Mentoree: I'm not sure if I have. If I do delegate, it will be difficult for me. I make no secret of that.

Mentor: If delegation is a problem, is it because of a fear of losing control, or do you not have anyone to whom to delegate?

Mentoree: Both, I suppose. You've heard the numbers. You've seen the set-up.

Mentor: It is something to be borne in mind when we examine that part of the business plan. As a "get to know you better" activity, do you organise any staff get-togethers?

Mentoree: For training?

Mentor: No. To celebrate an event, for example, a staff member's birthday, or the receipt of a significant order, or the achievement of a special production target to fill an urgent order.

Mentoree: We have a Christmas party. That is all. The other events you mentioned sound like a good idea. I have read about that type of event in some management book. I will talk to the production manager about it.

Mentor: And the marketing people?

Mentoree: Why them?

Mentor: Do you market internally?

Mentoree: How do you mean?

Mentor: As all staff interface at different levels with customers, each employee has a contribution to make to marketing. It seems, therefore, to make sense to acquaint them with the company's products, their benefits and functions. It is considered, also, that informing the staff about company developments gives them a feeling of ownership and generates more interest in achieving higher quality in every aspect of the business. Informing the employees about the company sparks more interest in the company and is another element in creating employee enthusiasm. Hence, some people would say that marketing starts internally.

Mentoree: I suppose so. Should the marketing department organise such events?

Mentor: I think so. Usually, they have the most experience of organising similar events. It seems to fit into their routine more easily. Also, it gives them an opportunity to make an internal promotion of a policy or to present some general information.

Mentoree: Yes, I can see the point. I will discuss it with my marketing person.

Mentor: To move on, if I may: another topic that is getting a lot of attention these days is the question of health and safety. Do you have a Health and Safety Policy and a Health and Safety Statement?

Mentoree: Yes. We have been in compliance with the law since its introduction. Maybe the Production Supervisor should join us for this part of our meeting.

Mentor: Yes, why not?

The Production Supervisor joins the meeting. The mentor reminds him of the purpose of the mentor programme and repeats that he, the mentor, is familiarising himself with all aspects of the business.

Mentor: We were discussing the company's Health and Safety programme.

**Production
Supervisor:** I went to a seminar about health and safety and was given a very good handout. I then gave a talk to all the employees, including the boss and his wife. Together, the boss and I drafted the company's Health and Safety Policy and Health and Safety Statement.

Mentor: There is more to health and safety than the policy and statement, isn't there?

Production

Supervisor: Yes. We have had the health and safety officer from the Agency here and he has been very helpful. I don't think we have a problem there. It is a matter of eternal vigilance.

The meeting has gone on for some time but the mentor wishes to cover some remaining points to ensure that he has a good overview of the business.

Mentor: Have you any plans for the premises? Do you intend to expand it or develop it in any way, or, possibly, move to another plant?

Mentoree: No immediate plans. We'll move when we have to.

Mentor: On present performance, when do think that will be?

Mentoree: I would say, in about three years. This is part of the planning again, isn't it?

Mentor: Yes, it is. Do you anticipate having to carry out any significant repairs in the meantime?

Production

Supervisor: Nothing out of the ordinary, maybe some painting.

Mentor: While the Production Supervisor is here, perhaps we should discuss some other topics. Do you have a list of machinery and equipment?

Mentoree: Yes. But where it is I don't know. I can easily make another one. I know I should have it in a special file.

Mentor: What about production equipment that you would like to have to improve quality, improve efficiency and increase productivity? Have you collected any data on possible purchases?

Mentoree: I know what would be beneficial but I don't have a list prepared. The Production Supervisor and I have had many discussions about this.

Mentor: Have you worked out the cost of such equipment?

Mentoree: Approximately. It is expensive, so I'm pretty sure that we will have to buy second-hand. Sourcing the equipment will also take some time.

Production
Supervisor: I could do that. It wouldn't take too much time.

Mentor: It would be helpful if you could get the delivered cost of equipment requirements also, and an estimate of the installation cost for inclusion in the cash budget part of the business plan. We must be sure that the purchases do not stretch the projected cash flow in the foreseeable future.

Mentoree: Is the projected cash flow statement a cash budget?

Mentor: Yes. I should have said that. It is part of your business plan. But it is the part that must be updated regularly. And we mustn't forget office equipment. Do you have a computer?

Mentoree: Yes.

Mentor: Is your computer new?

Mentoree: Nearly two years old.

Mentor: When do you plan to change it?

Mentoree: In about two years. That is the usual timeframe for computers, I believe.

Mentor: Does the company own or lease any motor vehicles, including forklifts or similar materials handling equipment?

Mentoree: We have one flatbed truck, just paid for, one car, for the marketing manager, I own mine, and then there is the forklift you saw inside. It was inside, when you walked around the factory, wasn't it?

Mentor: If it was, I didn't see it. Perhaps it was outside?

Mentoree: Maybe.

Mentor: Are all the vehicles in good order?

Production

Supervisor: Pretty well. The forklift may have to be changed, in about a year, the flatbed truck in two years. More planning, I suppose?

Mentor: Indeed. If the business expands as you expect, will you need any more motor vehicles or materials handling equipment?

Mentoree: I haven't thought about it. That is a bit more difficult to see.

Mentor: There seemed to be a lot of manhandling of materials in the factory. Is there some equipment that would do the work?

Production Supervisor: Undoubtedly there is, from heavy cranes to trolleys.

Mentoree: That raises all sorts of other questions. It is obviously linked to other factors, many of which have been mentioned today. I will look into it.

Mentor: I am not sure that we can do much more today about production.

Mentoree: In that case, we need not detain the Production Supervisor.

The mentor thanks the Production Supervisor for his contribution. The Production Supervisor leaves the office.

Mentor: I should like to talk to you about your accounting system and the reports it provides. You told me earlier that your wife looks after the accounts?

Mentoree: Yes. She writes up the books, sends out the invoices and statements and generally sees that the figures are correct. Perhaps we should ask my wife to join us, as we are talking about her side of the business.

The mentoree's wife comes into the office. She greets the mentor who explains to her how the mentoring programme works and that the purpose of the first meeting is to familiarise the mentor with all aspects of the business.

Mentoree's wife: When I heard that a mentor was coming this week, it was like taking a weight off my mind. My husband and I have been living this business 24 hours a day. We don't seem able to leave it here in the plant and have a normal life outside it. I hope that you will help us to bring a sense of proportion into our lives.

Mentor: Well, I will do my best to help in whatever way I can. Your husband and I have been looking at the possibility of drawing up a business plan with a view to providing better control over the progress of the business. I should say that many business gurus prefer to use the word "measurement" rather than "control". Delegation is another topic we discussed briefly. Both of these should provide you both with more free time. Before you came in, I was asking about the accounts and was just about to ask what month-end financial reports are prepared?

Mentoree's wife: I prepare an aged list of debtors, a list of creditors and the bank reconciliation.

Mentor: Do you prepare management accounts during the year?

Mentoree's wife: No. I don't feel competent to prepare them. The auditor prepares accounts at the end of the financial year.

Mentor: Do you prepare a projected cash flow statement, at anytime during the year?

Mentoree's wife: No, never. I have heard of them, of course, but I haven't seen one. But the bank manager always asks whether we have one when we pay him our annual visit.

Mentor: So you do not know whether you are making profits from one end of the year to the other?

Mentoree: That's correct. It means also that I am always nervous about buying new equipment. As a result, I always buy on lease. And very expensive it is too. I dare say my wife could learn how to prepare a cash flow projection, if she had the time.

Mentor: Preparing a household cash budget is something we all do, to some extent. A projected cash flow statement for your business is similar. We ask ourselves, what cash do I expect to collect from the debtors (receivables) and when, how much do I have to pay creditors (payables) and when, what is the difference and adjust my bank balance accordingly.

**Mentoree's
wife:**   Is there any way I can calculate whether we are making a profit, without going to the expense of asking our auditor?

Mentor: The only sure way is to prepare management accounts. In the absence of these, it is possible to prepare an estimate by comparing the current position with a previous current position, with some adjustments.

Mentoree: What is a current position?

Mentor: A current position is the difference between your current assets and your current liabilities. Let me illustrate.

The mentor reaches for his notepad and pencil and drafts a simple current position statement.

Figure 5.5: Current Position Statement

	€	€
Current Assets		
Stock	1,000	
Debtors	500	
Cash	200	
		1,700
Current Liabilities		
Trade Creditors	600	
Taxation	300	
		900
Current Position		**800**

Mentor: Would you mind if we left that for the moment? I promise to come back to it in another meeting.

Mentoree: Of course.

Mentor: One of the most important activities, if not the most important, of any business is the collection of cash. Do you look after credit control?

Mentoree's wife: Yes. Except when I am having a problem with an account. Then I call on my husband or pass the account to the marketing person.

Mentor: Do you decide on the credit terms applicable to each account?

Mentoree: To a degree. The marketing manager would decide on some. Frankly, we don't have a formal system of fixing credit limits. When we started the company, we were so grateful to companies for buying our product that we have been a bit slack in that regard.

Mentor: How about your stocks? Do you stock-take regularly, say, once a month?

Mentoree: We do have a partial stock-take every month, but only of the core raw materials. The smaller items we estimate, unless delivery time is likely to be long.

Mentor: Do you cost the stock-sheet each time?

Mentoree: No. It hasn't seemed to be necessary. Should I?

Mentor: It will be necessary to do so if you want to prepare a current position each month. I think that we might apply your present practice of stock-taking to stock-costing — that is, cost the core items and estimate the other items. It is something we will have to look at. Do you keep stock records on the computer?

Mentoree: No. We did try. I spoke to a few friends of mine who tried to maintain stock records on their computers, but it was so difficult, they gave up.

Mentor: It's not easy. Obviously some computer programs are better suited than others. By the way, there are a few other things that I think we should touch on to make sure that I have the full picture. They are not the liveliest topics but it would be foolhardy to plan without having all the facts. They deal with such matters as product insurance, insurances in general, the annual audit, your relations with the bank and, inevitably, taxation.

Mentoree: We have had product insurance since day one.

Mentor: Do you have keyman insurance?

Mentoree: No. We thought about it initially, but decided not to take it out as the business was a start-up and it didn't make much sense. I think now that you mention it, we should review that decision. What were the other ones?

Mentor: Consequential Loss Insurance. Do you have periodic meetings with your insurance broker?

Mentoree: Once a year. He takes me through the entire insurance schedule. Other matters you mentioned?

Mentor: The annual audit?

Mentoree: Completed last month. I like to have it finished within three months of the financial year-end.

Mentor: How do you get on with the bank?

Mentoree: We have our moments, but in general, we get on quite well.

Mentor: What is the position in respect of the company's tax liabilities?

Mentoree: To the best of my knowledge, we are up-to-date. Our auditor looks after that side of the business.

Mentor: Any problems with creditors?

Mentoree: No.

Mentor: The company is not being sued by anyone, is it?

Mentoree: No.

Mentor: And you are not suing anyone?

Mentoree: No.

Mentor: End of interrogation!

Mentoree: Thank you.

Before concluding the meeting, the mentor wishes to give the mentoree the opportunity to raise any matters not discussed.

Mentor: Is there anything else about the business that we have not considered?

Mentoree: I don't think so. We seem to have taken it apart.

Mentor: As you have seen, I have taken a lot of notes. I will give you a copy of them to make sure that we are both looking at the same business.

Mentoree: I've told you how it is.

Mentor: Have you heard of the "window test"?

Mentoree: No.

Mentor: Look out a window and write down ten things you see. Ask another person to look out the same window and tell you ten things they see. You write them down. And so on with other people. Then compare the lists you have made and pay particular attention to the order in which the various people listed the things they saw. You will be surprised at the differences and especially the differences in the order they saw things.

Mentoree: I get the point.

Mentor: Do you think that we have covered enough ground for this first meeting? What do you think?

Mentoree: I should say so.

There remains the agreement of tasks that the mentoree sees as necessary for him to complete before the next meeting to make it productive.

Mentor: Of the various topics requiring action that we discussed, which would you hope to tackle before our next meeting?

Mentoree: I really must begin work on the business plan. The marketing plan will be the starting point. There are so many other things to do that we have discussed. But, as you said, I must prioritise.

Mentor: Don't worry about the long list of topics we discussed. We will get to them all in due course. It seems to be a good idea to begin with the marketing plan. To start with it, it doesn't have to be perfect, just get some ideas down on paper. And don't forget the old saying, "The planning process is as important as the plan." The best marketing director I have met made prose notes in the first instance, and afterwards quantified his thoughts. Adjustments, rewriting, amendments, call them what you will, followed, until the final draft emerged. But don't forget the overall structure within which the marketing plan will fit. Your idea of prioritising the tasks is, in my view, excellent. What parts of the marketing plan will you start with?

Mentoree: I'd like to start with the product, the "Consumer's Prayer" that we talked about. Then I will divide the market for our product into segments. I will prioritise these segments. The next step should be to fix targets for these segments.

Mentor: How will you do that?

Mentoree: Within each segment, I will list potential customers and their potential purchases of our product.

Mentor: How will you promote your product to them?

Mentoree: The usual ways — letters, mail shots, telesales, sales calls, but, this time, I will follow your suggestion of quantifying marketing activity. I will note the number of letters to be sent, the number of mail shots, the number of phone calls to be made and the number of sales calls to be made.

Mentor: It might be helpful to list the channels of communication, personalised and non-personalised, not forgetting e-mail within the principles of permission marketing. Then, within the channels of communication selected, detail the activities you deem most appropriate to your business. Now, how many prospects do you need to have to produce one sale?

Mentoree: I don't know. I will have to discuss that with my marketing person. We will go over past sales figures and see if we can reconstruct the number of prospects we had at different times.

Mentor: When do you consider a contact a prospect?

Mentoree: When they ask for a demonstration of the product.

Mentor: So you will quantify marketing activity, calculate the number of prospects and from those estimate the number and amount of sales?

Mentoree: Yes. That is the idea.

Mentor: I usually illustrate that progression with the "Sales Pyramid".

The mentor, once again, draws a diagram on his notepad and hands it to the mentoree.

Figure 5.6: The Sales Pyramid

Mentor:	The objective is to move the people up the pyramid, the suspects to become prospects. A client is someone who buys once. As you know, a repeat order is what we all need. When the repeat order materialises, the client becomes a customer.
Mentoree:	What are "champions"?
Mentor:	They are clients who recommend your products to other potential purchasers. We can discuss the pyramid again. To move on, will you calculate what sales costs will be involved?
Mentoree:	Yes. These will largely be cost of sales literature, the cost of the phone calls and, of course, travelling expenses, not to mention salaries, commissions and such like.
Mentor:	In all that, you have the basic material of a marketing plan. When — not putting you under pressure, of course — do you expect to have a draft?
Mentoree:	In about six weeks' time.
Mentor:	Why don't we meet then?
Mentoree:	Perfect. Same time?

Mentor: Agreed.

The mentor puts his notes in his briefcase, rises, shakes hands with the mentoree's wife and the mentoree and leaves the office.

6

THE SECOND MEETING

The purpose of the second meeting is to review the work done by the mentoree and his management team since the previous session and, then, to agree the work to be done before the third meeting.

At the second meeting, the mentor discusses in more detail some of the topics touched upon previously. They were scheduled at the end of the first meeting for further discussion at the second meeting.

This chapter should be read in conjunction with *Figure 6.1*.

Figure 6.1: Agenda for the Second Meeting

Short review of the first meeting	The mentoree's thoughts about the first meeting are discussed and the objectives set at that meeting for the second meeting are reviewed. At subsequent meetings, the objectives for the meeting should be agreed before the review (cf. Minutes).
New Business	If a business does not have a steady stream of new business, eventually it will have no business. New business is usually considered under sub-headings such as New Customers (number and amount), Significant Business from Existing Customers, Quotations Outstanding.
Marketing	The marketing activity schedule, in which all marketing tasks are listed with targeted completion dates, is reviewed.
New Products/ Services/R&D	It is advisable to keep the continuing need for new products in focus, to avoid product obsolescence.

Projects in Progress	As in the first meeting, under this heading are listed activities with a short-term completion date such as the annual audit. Items remaining under this heading for longer than three months should be investigated.
Personnel	This heading can be subdivided — for example, into number by department, recruitment needs, resignations, training.
Premises	A review of the condition of the premises and any improvements necessary. The cash flow implications are obvious.
Transport	This heading can be subdivided — for example, into number by marque, type, mileage, age and function/requirements. The information will be reflected in the Cash Flow Projection.
Equipment	This heading can be divided into two: Production Equipment and Office Equipment. The condition of existing equipment and future needs are reviewed at every meeting. The implications for cash flow are obvious.
Finance	This heading can be subdivided — for example, into Profit and Loss Account for the period, Balance Sheet, Projected Cash Flow, Aged Debtors Schedule, Aged Creditors Schedule, Summarised and Classified Inventory.
Any Other Business	This provides an opportunity for the mentoree to talk about topics not specifically listed in the agenda, and for the mentor to raise matters that occur to him from the conversation up to this point.
Review of achievements of meeting	The mentor and mentoree assess the meeting primarily to see whether the objectives set out at the start of the meeting have been achieved.
Task for next meeting	The mentoree lists the task(s) that he intends to complete before the next meeting.
Date of next meeting	It is important to agree the date of the next meeting.

The mentor enters the managing director's office and greets the managing director and the marketing person. As the topics to be discussed centre on the marketing activities of the company, the managing director, by agreement with the mentor, had asked the marketing person to attend. The mentor takes out his notebook.

Mentoree: You met our marketing person at the last meeting.

Mentor: Yes. I am pleased to meet you again and hope you are enjoying our mentoring sessions.

Marketing person: Yes. I am looking forward to these discussions.

Mentoree: Now where do we start today?

Mentor: Well, how did things go?

Mentoree: Fairly mixed, frankly. No, that's not strictly true. At first, it was difficult, but, as things progressed, I felt that we were getting somewhere. But first, I decided, at least as an interim measure, to call the marketing person our "Marketing Executive". That seemed to clarify, to some extent, the function in my mind.

Mentor: I am glad that the decision was helpful. Can you be more specific about the difficulties you experienced?

Mentoree: Where to begin?

Mentor: Let me consult my notes. You said the last day that you would start with the "Consumer's Prayer", "Do not offer me things. Offer me ideas, emotions, ambience, feelings, benefits. Do not offer me tools. Offer me the benefit and pleasure of making beautiful things."

Mentoree: Yes, that is correct. For the life of me, I don't know why I said that I would do that. It was impossible. I struggled with it for two days and then gave up. I moved on to dividing the market into segments.

Mentor: Why do you think you found the "Consumer's Prayer" impossible?

Mentoree: I am not sure that I know where to start. Can you help me?

Mentor: Let me see. Do you have a sample of the product here? I think that we need a sample of the product, to inspire us.

Mentoree: I agree.

Mentor: I think it would be useful, also, to have the Production Supervisor present, if he is available.

Mentoree: Good idea. I will ask him to bring a sample twidget with him.

The Production Supervisor joins the meeting. He has a sample of the product. The managing director addresses him.

Mentoree: You met our mentor during his first visit here. We have just started to discuss the work we did on the marketing plan. The mentor suggested that we should ask you to join us so that we can examine the product together.

Production Supervisor: But I have nothing to do with the marketing plan. It is not my job or, at any rate, I don't think it is. Am I right?

Mentor: In general terms, you are not quite right about that. Everyone in the company has a part to play in marketing.

Production Supervisor: I still don't know what I have to do with marketing.

Mentor: Well, to give you one example. From the purely production point of view, it would not make sense for the marketing department to schedule sales and delivery dates in isolation. In the first place, they would need to consult the production department about the possibility of producing the products that the marketing department plans to sell.

Production
Supervisor: I can see that all right.

Mentor: And, apart from the ability of the production department to produce the products, the question of
timing of production has to be considered.

Production
Supervisor: That makes sense.

Mentor: The aim is to create customer satisfaction, isn't it?

Production
Supervisor: Yes.

Mentor: Producing a quality product with on-time delivery
is a significant part of creating customer satisfaction. Isn't that your function? And you probably
have some face-to-face interaction with customers?

Production
Supervisor: Yes, I do. I see the connection now.

Mentor: What we are hoping to do today, as a first step, is to
look again at the product to see whether we can list
its benefits for the user.

Mentoree: Is it correct to ask ourselves, at this point, why we
make the product at all?

Mentor: Very much so. I think you told me that the product
was developed to supply a gap in the market, or so
I understand.

Mentoree: Not exactly. There was — is — a product manufactured by another company to fill a niche in the
market. That other product is still sold. Now, there
are several manufacturers of similar products. I
developed an improved version.

Mentor: Your version provides additional benefits for the
user?

Mentoree: Yes, you could say that.

Production
Supervisor: This approach is all new to me.

Mentor: Can you tell me why anyone would want to use this
product?

Production

Supervisor: This twidget, in the first instance, removes the un-even edging of a fabrication and then coats a specific part or indeed, if required, the entire fabrication with whatever protective and/or decorative substance is appropriate.

Mentor: That describes the functionality of the product. What is the benefit to the user?

Production

Supervisor: I thought I've just told you that. Manufacturers of many types of products use the twidget in their manufacturing process. It is not a High Street product. I still don't follow what you are getting at. Can you give me a hint?

Mentor: The manufacturer you speak of, is he the end user? Perhaps his customer is the end-user? Does it help him, the manufacturer, to produce a better product?

Production

Supervisor: If it didn't, no one would use it.

Mentor: Could we then say "Don't offer me a twidget. Offer me more efficient production."?

Mentoree: It seems to me, that you are asking us to identify the benefits of the product.

Mentor: To some extent, but not entirely. Remember, "Do not offer me furniture. Offer me comfort and the quietness of a cosy place."

Marketing

Executive: "Do not offer me records. Offer me leisure and the sound of music." You see, I have done some homework!

Mentor: That's what makes my task so enjoyable. Thank you. Can you visualise what the manufacturer is thinking, in that manner, when he is looking for a product like yours?

Mentoree: "Do not offer me twidgets. Offer me . . ." It still seems to come back to the benefits of the product to the end-user, who is our customer.

Mentor: It is, of course, necessary to list the benefits of the product and how these benefits compare with those of competing products. You can then translate them into the "Consumer's Prayer". Can you do that?

Mentoree: The Production Supervisor and I can try, certainly. If cost is a factor, we have a problem because we are slightly more expensive than the competitors that we are aware of.

Mentor: Does your product have any unique features?

Production Supervisor: Oh, it does. It is, as I think you were told earlier, a more advanced product.

Mentor: Do these unique features justify the higher price, a premium price?

Marketing Executive: We think so. And more importantly, our customers seem to think so.

Mentor: Have you asked them?

Marketing Executive: No. I have always believed that customers vote with their purchase orders. We have never conducted a customer satisfaction survey, if that is what you are asking.

Mentoree: I think those surveys just encourage the customers to complain.

Marketing Executive: What do you think?

Mentor: I would prefer to hear customer's complaints sooner rather than later. That way, I can take remedial action before the situation is irrecoverable. But I am not pushing this activity. The decision is yours.

Mentoree: Fair enough. For my part, I will think about it again and consult in-house.

Mentor: Do you think that the differentiation of your product from competing products gives you a competitive advantage?

Marketing Executive: Today, I do. But it is something that I have to keep under review. So many issues are being raised here today that I need time to think about them.

Mentoree: The product is used only as part of a particular process in manufacturing. Is that an advantage or a disadvantage?

Mentor: There are elements of both in it. Could you say, as a competitive advantage, that the product has focus?

Mentoree: Yes, it is focused on a particular manufacturing process, in a particular industry. I agree with the Marketing Executive. We need time to think again about these ideas. Do you mind if I suggest that we move on? Suffice to say that we have more work to do on the "Consumer's Prayer".

Production Supervisor: Do you need me any more? May I get back to the product line? I'd better think of how to produce more to meet the extra demand you are obviously planning.

Mentor: Of course. Thank you for your assistance.

The Production Supervisor shakes hands with the mentor, picks up the sample twidget and leaves the managing director's office.

Mentoree: What now? Are we in a position to continue, or must we postpone further discussion until we have solved the question of product benefits and the "Consumer's Prayer"?

Mentor: No, I don't think so. When you have your marketing meeting do you produce statistics about sales achieved, number of new customers acquired since the last meeting and such like?

**Marketing
Executive:** We certainly talk about sales since our last meeting.

Mentor: And new customers?

**Marketing
Executive:** No, unless of particular interest. I suppose we should note all new customers.

Mentor: How about setting targets for the acquisition of new customers?

**Marketing
Executive:** Great and small?

Mentor: Exactly. And in a timeframe too — so many within a specified period.

**Marketing
Executive:** When I said great and small, I was partly joking. How are we to decide rationally the number of "great" as compared to "small"?

Mentor: Businesses that have given some thought to this approach divide their existing customers into groups depending on their sales history or their sales potential — for example, they have classifications such as platinum, gold, silver, bronze.

**Marketing
Executive:** And these classifications signify different levels of sales or sales potential?

Mentor: Yes. It is up to each business to decide at what level of sales a customer qualifies for what classification. The object is, of course, to try and promote customers up to the next level.

Mentoree: It prioritises them too, should we have supply problems. I think we should look at that.

The mentor thinks it is time to move on to the next related topic, which links activities to quantified goals and achievements.

Mentor: We can continue our discussions about classifying the customers when you have had time to think about it. Can we deal now with the marketing activities relevant to your product and appropriate for the size of your business? Did you list the marketing activities you thought would be most effective for your business?

Marketing Executive: We discussed what we have been doing in terms of marketing activity and what we think we should add.

Mentor: Did you make a list?

Marketing Executive: Yes. The list is long enough, covering written communications, direct contact, public relations and general housekeeping activities.

Mentor: I like the way you classify the marketing activities. Can you break them down for me, starting with the written communications?

Mentoree: The written communications include every form of contact by means of paper. These would include festival cards at Christmas and Easter and, maybe, summer. There are the usual letters, fliers, and we send copies of magazine articles that may be of interest to customers. We regard small promotional gifts like pens, writing pads, mats for cups or glasses and so forth as part of written communications. There are, also, competitions for customers and prospective customers and customer satisfaction questionnaires.

Mentor: Presumably you include in written communications contact by fax and e-mail?

Marketing Executive: Of course.

Mentor: How likely is it that you will do all these things?

Marketing
Executive: I don't know at this moment. At first, we listed everything we already do and then what we would like to do. It may be that we will plan to do them all over a few years. On the other hand, we may find that some of them are more effective than others and we will concentrate our efforts on those.

Mentor: And you mentioned direct contacts?

Marketing
Executive: Yes. There are direct contacts with customers and prospective customers. These include calling at their premises, phone calls, giving product demonstrations, breakfasts, lunches and dinners. In addition, we provide some training courses for users. We call them "product knowledge seminars".

Mentor: What sort of back-up do you visualise for all these activities?

Mentoree: As I told you last day, we have taken on an assistant for the marketing executive.

Mentor: What back-up activities will the marketing assistant carry out?

Marketing
Executive: Updating the database, phoning prospects to make appointments for visits to their premises or arranging demonstrations, sending the direct mail and filing reports and such like.

Mentor: The third classification you mentioned earlier was "general activities". What are those?

Marketing
Executive: The general activities include updating the database of customers and prospects, regular reviews of marketing report content and format, market research, competition analysis, documenting competitive advantage and regular reviews of the product benefits document. We also engage in some public relations and advertising.

Mentor: With so many possible activities to consider, it might be helpful for deciding which ones to focus on if the activities were divided between personalised and non-personalised communication channels. To some extent, you have done so by dividing the communications between direct and indirect.

Mentoree: I can see that such analysis could save time ultimately.

Mentor: Do you do any complaints analysis?

Marketing Executive: I am not quite sure what you mean. We don't have many complaints.

Mentoree: But we do have some.

Mentor: Who deals with the complaints?

Marketing Executive: I do.

Mentor: What are the complaints about?

Marketing Executive: They vary. Sometimes, they are about product faults. Other times, they are about late deliveries. On other occasions, they are about incorrect invoicing.

Mentoree: Once or twice a customer said that the product did not agree with the specification, but that was nonsense. What has this to do with sales budgeting?

Mentor: Every activity in the business and every customer response or reaction affects the achievement of sales budget targets. Have you ever lost a customer as a result of a complaint?

Mentoree: Yes. It's rare, but we have on occasion.

Mentor: How did that come about?

Mentoree: In one case, the customer phoned in a complaint. My wife took the call. She passed it to me and to the Marketing Executive. I thought the Marketing Executive was dealing with it. She thought I was dealing with it. Nothing was done. The customer became very irritated at what he saw as a "couldn't care less" attitude, returned the product and has refused to deal with us since then.

Mentor: Do you keep in touch with that customer?

Marketing Executive: Ex-customer. He is on our mailing list and is sent fliers occasionally.

Mentor: Do you think that that is enough?

Marketing Executive: Perhaps not. What do you suggest?

Mentor: I have heard of a similar case in another company. A complaint was, inadvertently, ignored. The customer was outraged. The managing director of the company called to see his opposite number in the aggrieved company and was roundly abused. He than let some time pass. He called again. He received somewhat less abuse this time. After a few such visits, receiving less and less criticism each time, he was given another order. Is there a moral to this story?

Mentoree: Which of us should contact the customer?

Mentor: Do you think that it would be more impressive if both of you called on your former customer?

Marketing Executive: I think so.

Mentoree: I agree.

Mentor: Do you think, now, that "complaints analysis" should be included in the marketing activities, under the classification "general"?

Marketing Executive: Point taken.

Mentor: If you like, I will draw up a complaints form for you. It should ensure that the complaint does not get overlooked because of confusion about who is responsible for dealing with it.

Mentoree: Please.

The mentor draws on his pad the layout of a complaints form and hands it to the mentoree. He examines it and passes it to the Marketing Executive.

Figure 6.2: Complaint Report

Complaint from:	Tel.:
Address:	

Nature of Complaint:

Investigation of complaint by:	Date:

Corrective action by:	Date:

Preventative action by:	Date:

Report to customer by:	Date:

Supervisor 's signature:	Date:

Mentor: Returning to the listing of priorities, have you developed any overview of what the main thrust of the marketing activities will be?

Marketing
Executive: As I mentioned earlier, we will try to carry out all the activities mentioned, subject to further consideration, discussions with my assistant and, of course, a review with the managing director. I will take on board your suggestion about dividing

communication channels between personalised and non-personalised.

Mentoree: I will be available, also, to help with the marketing.

Mentor: So, you will both try to follow through on the marketing activities — written communications, direct contact and general?

Marketing Executive: Yes. We will do the best we can.

Mentor: That is quite a list. Can you carry out all those activities?

Marketing Executive: That remains to be seen. As I have mentioned several times, I have a new assistant in my department. That should make it possible to do more than previously. Together, we have partially prioritised the activities, but we may change the priorities as the plan develops.

Mentor: Have you a time plan for all these activities?

Marketing Executive: We are drafting a marketing activity schedule to test the feasibility of carrying out the tasks within a reasonable period, taking into account the resources available.

Mentor: You are quantifying the planned activities?

Marketing Executive: To some extent, that is, in the high priority activities. Before we finish, we hope to quantify all marketing activities. I recognise that quantification is necessary to evaluate the best use of marketing resources.

Mentor: Are you providing for a record of activities actually achieved?

Marketing Executive: Absolutely. I know that we need a record of activities completed to measure progress against plan.

Mentor: How will you relate quantified activities planned to the sales budget?

Marketing Executive: I don't know. It isn't that we haven't thought of it. We liked your idea of quantifying marketing activities but we couldn't see the connecting link between the activities and the sales other than that the activities would or should yield sales.

Mentor: What is the objective of the marketing activities?

Marketing Executive: To make sales.

Mentor: Immediately?

Marketing Executive: No. Experience has shown that prospective customers will want to be given a demonstration of the product before they will buy. We call them demos.

Mentor: How many prospective customers do you need to produce one demo?

Marketing Executive: Oh. Let me see. On average, I would expect to achieve two demos for every ten prospects, that is, one in five. That is an improvement compared to a year ago. I doubt if we will do much better than that.

Mentor: Approximately how many demos does it take to produce one sale?

Marketing Executive: I will have to check the records. I think the figure is likely to be four.

Mentor: What do these figures tell us?

Marketing Executive: Let me see. To make one sale, we have to give four demos. One demo requires five prospects. So, four demos require 20 prospects. You could say, then, that every 20 prospects should produce one sale.

Mentor: On this basis, if you want to sell, say, 100 units in a financial period, you need 2,000 prospects, leading to 400 demonstrations to give you the unit sales required in that period. That is the numerical link between the marketing activities and the sales budget. Can you think of deviations from these statistics?

Marketing Executive: Well, of course. For example, on occasion, a new customer buys because they have seen the product being used by one of our customers. And our existing customers have to be taken into account. Also, there is another consideration, the size of each order varies considerably.

Mentor: Those examples you have just mentioned of other factors affecting the statistics, and there are bound to be others, can be taken into account in your planning. But please don't think that this approach is an exact science. It isn't. However, it does provide a useful methodology.

Marketing Executive: Market trends can alter figures up and down, of course.

Mentor: Indeed, they can. The art of the process, from your point of view, is to calculate what allowance you should make to take account of the current trends and the anticipated trends.

Marketing Executive: We shouldn't forget that product development could have a significant influence on the sales budget, not to say actual sales.

Mentoree: What about the competition? Shouldn't we take into consideration what they are likely to do?

Mentor: Undoubtedly. Your market research will include the gathering of information about the competition.

Marketing Executive: The perennial question is "How much information?"

Mentor: The more knowledge you have of your competitors' character and motivation, the more likely you are to predict their actions. And, of course, you must provide for possible changes in the character and motivation of the competition.

Mentoree: How will we know if that is likely to happen?

Mentor: The changes can result from a range of events, such as a change of the management of the competition or from events in the market. And we shouldn't forget that your own activities in the market might influence the actions of your competitors.

Mentoree: I can see that there is a logical sequence about the marketing activity. We start with market research, consider a range of possible sales targets, identify prospects, list and quantify marketing activities to persuade prospects to attend demos and proceed through demos to convert the prospects into customers and thus achieve the agreed sales targets.

Mentor: That is the process. But continuing vigilance is essential for two reasons. Firstly, to be aware quickly of any change of trend in the market. Secondly, to be sensitive to any easing in sales demand, not just generally, but in the case of individual existing customers. And don't forget the use of time series statistical models. They compute the trend of past sales allowing for any seasonality and, on the basis of the trend shown, forecast future sales. There are software packages that do it for you and they are user-friendly.

Mentoree: Even with all this, and I don't want you to think that I am being negative, it is impossible to know which activity or activities produce the results.

Mentor: That is correct. As Lucretius said, "Happy the man who has learned the causes of things."

Mentoree: For how long should a marketing activity be tried, before it is clear whether it is effective or not?

Mentor: I don't know. In general, I can say that business people tend to become impatient if results don't come quickly. I advise perseverance with each activity for the planned period of that activity. Also, it is essential to maintain the agreed level of the activity during that period. That is the best way to really test the effectiveness of a marketing activity.

Marketing Executive: I agree. Persistence and consistency are the by-words.

Mentor: You talked earlier about prospects. How do you define a prospect?

Marketing Executive: A prospect is a company that we identify as a potential user of our product and which we contact, initially, by letter, flier and telephone.

Mentor: When you contact them by phone, must they express an interest in the product in order to continue to be classified as a prospect?

Marketing Executive: Not necessarily. If they don't state categorically that they do not have any interest in the product, and are never likely to have any interest in the product, they remain prospects.

Mentor: Do you make any distinction among prospects?

Mentoree: How do you mean?

Mentor: At any given time, don't you deem some prospects closer to a purchase than others?

Mentoree: Certainly, and those that are get more attention.

Mentor: Naturally. Presumably those closer to purchase are fewer in number than those not so close?

Mentoree: Yes.

Mentor: Could you classify those as "probables"?

Mentoree: Yes, indeed.

Mentor: You could say we now have the foundation of a pyramid of classifications. At the base, there are those on the database, sometimes called suspects. Next there are the prospects, a smaller number. Then there are the probables, still fewer in number.

Mentoree: What are "suspects"?

Mentor: Oh, sorry. Suspects are people or businesses that are not aware of your existence, or that know of your existence but do not know what you produce. Who do you think form the next layer of the pyramid?

Mentoree: The clients, I suppose.

Mentor: Exactly. The next layer is made up of the end results of much of this activity, those who buy, the clients. That might seem to be the lot, but there are others. Can you suggest any others?

Mentoree: Yes, you told me about another classification. Clients who give repeat orders are classified as customers.

Mentor: Yes. They occupy the next tier in the pyramid. Now we come to the final layer. Have you any idea who they might be?

Mentoree: Yes. You gave them the title of champions.

Mentor: Exactly. If you are lucky, some of your clients and customers will recommend your product to other potential users. They are usually easily counted, unfortunately, and occupy the top of the pyramid. They are called, as you said, champions. Every business loves to have champions.

Mentoree: Presumably there is a purpose in this type of classification?

Mentor: Yes, there is. You recall that we linked the marketing activities to the sales budget?

Mentoree: Yes.

Mentor: The pyramid classification is an aid to arriving at a more credible sales budget. Using the statistical process we talked about (you recall that 20 prospects were required for every sale), the aim is to

progress up the pyramid quantifying the classification on each layer of it.

Figure 6.3: The Sales Pyramid

Mentoree: How does the pyramid help marketing activity?

Mentor: You use it to help you to decide how much of each
marketing activity to allocate to each layer of the
pyramid.

Mentoree: Can you be a bit more specific?

Mentor: You decide, for example, how many letters and fliers you will send to prospects, how many follow-up
phone calls you will make to them. The probables
are those who have been to a demo and have expressed an interest in the product. You decide
what marketing activities you allocate to them. The
same goes for clients, customers and champions.
Don't forget that, when suspects become prospects, new suspects must replace them.

Mentoree: You said that sales budgeting is not an exact science.

Mentor: Absolutely. But that doesn't mean that we shouldn't
use every technique available to calculate, to the
best of our ability, a realistic sales budget. As you
know, the rest of the business plan is dependent on

the sales budget, and the future of the company is based on actual sales.

Mentoree: There is quite a bit of work in all this?

Mentor: Yes, but it is fascinating work. And when the marketing budget is agreed, there is the task of meeting the targets decided. How do we progress from here?

Marketing Executive: It seems to me that the first thing to do is select the marketing activities most appropriate to our needs and resources.

Mentor: Exactly. What then?

Marketing Executive: The next step is to allocate the chosen marketing activities to the different layers of the pyramid.

Mentor: I agree. What is next?

Marketing Executive: The delegation of the activities to the people available here in the company is the next logical step.

Mentoree: How does the pyramid relate to the classification of customers?

Mentor: As you can see from the pyramid, the customers are on the fifth level. The classification of the customers is made at that level. Within that level, marketing activities are dedicated to moving the customers from one classification to a higher one.

Mentoree: Should we now talk about what all this will cost?

Mentor: It seems to be the appropriate time to have, at least, a first look at the expenses involved. We can't, I think, be too specific about costs without the details of the marketing activity being agreed. But, to agree the extent of the marketing activities, it is necessary to have an idea of the order of magnitude of the likely costs of those activities. Costs will set a limit on the extent of the activities.

Mentoree: There is an element of backwards and forwards about this process.

Mentor: You could say that. It is more pronounced the first time that you prepare a budget. Afterward, with the experience gained, the process is more rapid.

Mentoree: Are we likely to arrive at a workable budget, given that this is our first attempt at preparing one in a comprehensive manner?

Mentor: I have heard it said that it takes "three bites of the apple" to establish not only an achievable budget, but also a credible budgeting process.

Mentoree: I see. Now will we look at the costs?

Marketing Executive: Could you give us some idea of the costs that would be classified "marketing expenses"?

Mentor: They vary from business to business. I usually distinguish between marketing costs and sales costs. Marketing costs include marketing personnel costs, advertising, public relations, letters, fliers, travelling costs of marketing personnel, entertainment, and communications, including sales literature, the cost of catalogues, to mention just a few.

Mentoree: And the sales expenses?

Mentor: Once again, sales personnel costs including commissions, communications in the form of telesales, travelling costs of sales personnel, special discounts and rebates and the cost of price lists.

Mentoree: Those classifications are very general. For example, what do personnel costs include?

Mentor: You are right. They are very general. Personnel costs include salaries, bonuses, commissions, pension contributions, health insurance contributions, travel awards, training and, where applicable, clothes allowances.

Mentoree: And communications?

Mentor: Communications costs can be quite varied. Firstly, communications costs are split between marketing and selling. Within both categories, I would expect communications costs to include stationery, printing, postage, telephone, mobile telephone, fax and e-mail.

Mentoree: Would you include the cost of catalogues and price lists in communications costs?

Mentor: No. Catalogues are usually very costly. I would list them separately under marketing expenses. I would list the cost of price lists separately under selling expenses. However, I recognise that some executives would include price lists with catalogues.

Mentoree: I can see confusion arising as different people are likely to classify expenses somewhat differently.

Mentor: That can happen. To avoid confusion, it is advisable to have a glossary of expense headings and how they are to be classified. Consistency in classification of expenses is essential if comparisons of budgeted expenses with actual expenses incurred are to have any usefulness.

Mentoree: Do you think that we have the knowledge to draft the glossary?

Mentor: You certainly have sufficient knowledge to make a start. Our discussions today should be helpful. If you have problems, we can discuss them at our next meeting, or you could consult your auditor.

Marketing Executive: If we complete the tasks outlined today, is the sales budget process finished?

Mentor: No. I mentioned earlier the linkage of marketing activities to sales. But linkage goes further than marketing activities. A critical factor in the linkage process is staff training. I think we talked about that at our last meeting. In many cases, the linkage between staff training and sales is direct and quantifiable. To take a simple example, an average sales representative achieves a certain level of sales, the actual level depending on the industry. An apprentice salesperson s achieves a lower level of sales. A training programme will improve the apprentice's sales ability. The expected improvement can be estimated, drawing on past experience of similar training courses and the results achieved.

Mentoree: Is the relationship of sales training to sales the only linkage that is relevant?

Mentor: No. If shortage of production personnel is impeding sales, training of a specific number of new production recruits will facilitate sales by a quantifiable amount. Training schedules will enable production management to give a time plan for increasing production.

Mentoree: What next?

Mentor: The next step is to set up a monitoring procedure. Do you have any thoughts about how you would go about a monitoring procedure?

Marketing Executive: From my point of view, the achievement of sales is paramount. I dare say that the budget is the plan that must be achieved.

Mentor: I agree. Monitoring sales compared to budget is essential. Will you monitor anything else?

Marketing Executive: I will monitor all the marketing activities we decide to engage in and compare them to our agreed schedule of marketing activity.

Mentoree: Do I have a part to play in all this?

Mentor: Yes. You co-ordinate the agreement of the budget by all department heads, not forgetting the underlying linkage of training and processes to sales. After that agreement, the most important part of the budgeting process is the commitment of all parties to it. The budget is a plan. It is not a wish list.

Mentoree: How can I be sure that everyone involved is committed?

Mentor: When you are all satisfied that the budget is doable, I recommend that you sign and date the front page of the budget document. Each department head will sign the section of the budget for which they are responsible.

Mentoree: Is that not a bit formal for a small business like ours?

Mentor: It may seem unduly formal for a small business but it does focus all concerned on the tasks they have accepted. And another thing, with this planning process you are not going to remain small. If systems, albeit simple ones, are put in place now you will avoid the trauma of putting them in place when the business is much larger. As they say, "If you want to be big, think big."

Mentoree: But, so far, we have been talking about the sales budget only.

Mentor: That is correct. The same procedure will be applied to the budget for each department of the business. The departmental budgets are, of course, interconnected and will be integrated into the total budget for the business.

Mentoree: You mean that the department budgets are interdependant?

Mentor: Yes. It follows that individual department budgets cannot be finally agreed until it is clear that all departmental budgets co-ordinate with one another. Can you think of anything else that should be done to ensure the achievement of the budget?

Mentoree: Make sure that we don't forget that it exists!

**Marketing
Executive:** I have a feeling that the sales budget won't be forgotten, whatever about the others.

Mentor: Yes, of course there is that danger. How do you propose to make sure that that does not happen?

Mentoree: Regular meetings?

Mentor: Yes. That is necessary. But, how many people are we relying on to achieve the budget?

Mentoree: The department heads and myself, of course, that is the marketing executive and the production supervisor and I, three in all.

Mentor: What about the accounts department? Does it not have an important monitoring function apart, altogether, from achieving its own budget objectives?

Mentoree: Now that you mention it, should my wife join us for this part of the discussion?

Mentor: I think so.

The mentoree's wife joins the meeting. The mentor gives her a summary of the discussions so far and explains why she has been asked to join the meeting. He answers her questions and confirms that she is satisfied she has been brought up-to-date.

Mentoree's Wife: Now that I have been brought up-to-date, please tell me what are the accounts department's responsibilities in the budgeting process?

Mentor: To record the transactions of the business in a manner that enables comparison with the budget. That will involve some detailed analysis, for example, of marketing and sales costs. Do you agree with that?

Mentoree's Wife: I thought that finance was the driving force of every business.

Mentor: That used to be the view. Then marketing was regarded as the driving force of a business. Now, as we discussed at our last meeting, a combination of marketing and R&D is viewed as the driver of an enterprise. All other activities — production, dis-

tribution, finance and administration — are regarded as support functions. What does that suggest to you?

Mentoree: That the support functions could be out-sourced?

Mentor: Exactly.

Mentoree: That seems a bit drastic.

Mentor: Indeed, it is. But, in practice, only some of a company's functions are out-sourced. But that is not
something we are discussing today. Do you think
that anyone else should be involved in achieving
the budget?

**Marketing
Executive:** I think that my assistant should be involved.

Mentoree: In the planning?

**Marketing
Executive:** Not in the planning as such, as we have been doing, but in agreeing the quantification of the various marketing activities that we select. After all, it
would not make any sense to set activity targets
that are impossible to achieve.

Mentoree: Is that all?

**Marketing
Executive:** No. I think it would be advisable, also, to agree the
time-plan for the marketing activities.

Mentor: Will you explain to your assistant the reasons for
having a plan and how the marketing activities play
a fundamental role in it?

**Marketing
Executive:** Of course. I would expect to go into the detail of
the marketing budget, and, to a lesser extent, the
overall budget, so my assistant can see where
marketing fits into the total budget. I have been
reading about the linkage of activity and results.
One thing I thought was significant was the advisability of giving sufficient information to employees
to enable them to achieve optimum productivity.

Mentor: Should anyone else be involved?

Mentoree: The Marketing Executive has made a very good point. After all, the budget requires everyone's support.

Mentor: Should the others, then — for example, the production operatives — be involved?

Mentoree: I think so.

Mentor: How involved?

Mentoree: I am not sure.

Mentor: You have overall responsibility for the budget. Do you agree?

Mentoree: Of course.

Mentor: The department heads have responsibility for their department budget. Isn't that right?

Mentoree: Yes.

Mentor: The Marketing Executive is involving the Marketing Assistant, to the extent that the Marketing Assistant can influence the achievement of the budget. But the Marketing Executive will give the Marketing Assistant an overview of the objectives of the budget and the Marketing Assistant's function in the overall budget. Isn't that correct?

**Marketing
Executive:** Yes. I would expect that knowing one's part in achieving the total objective would make the Marketing Assistant's job more interesting and more focused.

Mentoree: I can see that.

Mentor: Would the same apply to the production operatives?

Mentoree: It should do. How much detail should one give them?

Mentor: The Marketing Executive has defined the extent of the detail to be given to each person in the company.

Marketing
Executive: I see what you mean. Give a global view of the budget to provide focus on where each job, their own job, fits into the plan. From that, I would expect them to develop a greater interest in the tasks for which they are responsible.

Mentoree: I suppose each department head should inform his or her respective assistants?

Mentor: Yes, as far as the detail of each person's job is concerned. Do you think that, before doing that, a general presentation of the budget should be made to all the employees at a company-wide meeting?

Mentoree: To create a spirit of co-operation?

Mentor: Yes, to develop a team approach to its achievement. Who do you think should manage the presentation?

Mentoree: The Marketing Executive.

Mentor: Will you play a part?

Mentoree: That, I think, is a question for the Marketing Executive.

Mentor: It is part of internal marketing. How would you manage the presentation?

Marketing
Executive: I am sure that the Managing Director should launch the presentation with a few words. Then I would make the presentation of the budget. This would be followed by a short question-and-answer session. After that, there should be a small reception, a type of launching celebration.

Mentor: When will the department heads talk to their assistants about their individual tasks?

Mentoree: That should happen the following day, I think.

Mentor: That seems to me a very good approach. In the days and months that follow the budget launch, the employees will be interested to know how they are progressing compared to budget. What sort of report-back system would be the most effective?

Mentoree: I think that that will vary from department to department. The simpler, the better. It is our job to concentrate on the detail.

Mentor: What particular type of information would you give them?

Mentoree: I would give them information about the progress of their department. I would tell them how the business as a whole is doing compared to budget. I would tell them about our view of business prospects in the immediate future.

Mentor: How often would you give the information?

Mentoree: I think that information about their department should be given every week.

Mentor: And the business as a whole?

Mentoree: I think that that information should be given every month.

Mentor: When would you give your views about business prospects?

Mentoree: Annually.

Mentor: Would you have a reception every time?

Mentoree: No. Just monthly and annually.

The mentor is aware that a lot of material has been discussed and does not wish to overload the mentoree. He decides to touch briefly on a few topics to prepare the mentoree for future meetings.

Mentor: I would like to mention briefly a few matters you might like to think about for future meetings. The first is to do with personnel. We mentioned training and giving information, essential factors in personnel enthusiasm, productivity and retention. Another factor is recognition by means of a suggestion scheme. Working conditions are also important.

Mentoree: I will make a note of those.

Mentor: It is usual to review such matters as the premises, the equipment, the motor fleet, office equipment and any other asset the company has or requires. For the moment, we have discussed finance in terms of the budget but not cash management or profitability.

Mentoree: I think we should adopt the principle of "the inevitability of gradualness."

Mentor: Do you think that we have covered enough ground for this meeting?

Mentoree: Yes, I think so. It has been most interesting. As we progressed, many of the difficulties were reduced to a manageable size. Some were overcome or seemed to disappear. Preparing for the next meeting will not be so daunting or, at least, I don't think so.

Marketing Executive: There is a lot to do. If I feel overwhelmed, I will think of the linkage and the overall scheme of things. That should be calming.

Mentoree's Wife: I am glad to have been here because I too see the connection between the activities and I look forward to enjoying being part of the whole plan.

Mentor: What will you consider for the next meeting?

Mentoree: Whatever it is, it should follow on in a logical way. From our earlier discussions about linking the preliminary sales budget to production, I think that we should have a first look at the production needs to meet the sales budget. From that, we will have to look at the resources necessary to produce the product.

Mentor: Resources?

Mentoree: Yes. Have we enough equipment to produce the product when it is required? Do we need to recruit more people to operate any extra equipment purchased, or to assist with packing and distribution? And, of course there is the question of cash.

Mentor: Cash?

Mentoree: Yes. We will need cash to finance any equipment purchased, or, indeed, to help with the operation of existing equipment, to pay any extra wages, to finance any extra raw material bought, to finance any other incremental expenses and to finance the extra debtors.

Mentor: And linkage of goals and activities?

Mentoree: Of course.

Mentor: I must emphasise that, when we get to the cash budget or projected cash flow, we may have to have a rethink. To avoid a major alteration of plans, I suggest that, before the business plan becomes more advanced, we spend some time at our next meeting calculating the cash parameters within which you have to operate.

Mentoree's Wife: That solves one of my worries. I was afraid that we were rushing into something without calculating the cost and cash available.

Mentor: Very good. Shall we meet again in, say, six weeks?

Mentoree: Yes. That should give me adequate time to prepare.

Mentor: Did you find it useful having a copy of the notes I took the last day?

Mentoree: Very useful.

Mentor: Would you like to take a photocopy of the notes I made today?

Mentoree: Yes, please.

The mentoree takes a photocopy of the mentor's notes. The mentor shakes hands with all present and takes his leave.

7

ORGANISATION OF A MENTOR PROGRAMME

From time to time, organisations may wish to set up a Mentor Programme to promote the stability and, hopefully, the development of new and existing small and medium-sized enterprises, but are not sure how to go about it. These organisations may be government departments, state organisations, local authorities, trade associations, charitable institutions, artistic societies or corporate groups.

The type of Mentor Programme dealt with in this book is directed at the owners and/or managers of small and medium-sized entities, be they business units or non-profit-making societies.

These smaller organisations comprise the majority of businesses and artistic and charitable associations in every country. Large businesses usually can afford to employ consultants to achieve similar goals, which the small business or society would find prohibitively expensive.

OBJECTIVES AND FOCUS

Having decided to launch a mentor initiative, the first task for the promoters is to draft a mission statement and decide on the objectives of the programme. The goals set should be achievable with a reasonable amount of effort so that they are seen to be attainable by the majority of entrepreneurs accepted into the programme.

This may rule out setting such ambitious targets as an increase in employment, improvement in profitability, or development of new products or services. These objectives may be laudable in themselves but may be unattainable by many entrepreneurs because of the limitation of resources, human or financial, available to them.

It may not be advisable even to aim at the continuance in business of an enterprise, where it is clearly doomed for ineradicable reasons.

Prudence may suggest that the programme's main objective be to assist entrepreneurs to make the best use of their existing resources, human and financial, and generally improve their commercial performance.

As was seen earlier, within the broad scope of the goals defined for the programme, more detailed and specific targets will be set for mentor assignments in individual firms, taking into consideration their size and their current potential managerial ability.

The focus of a mentor programme is the mentoree and the mentor. To provide optimum benefits to the participants, a level of administration — one might almost say bureaucracy — is necessary.

In later sections of this chapter, we suggest report content for various activities in the programme. These can be altered to suit the particular circumstances of individual programmes.

ORGANISATION STRUCTURE

The structure of an organisation managing a Mentor Programme is relatively simple. It comprises a supervisory board, a programme director, regional co-ordinators, administrative staff and, of course, a panel of mentors.

Figure 7.1: Organisation Structure for a Mentor Programme

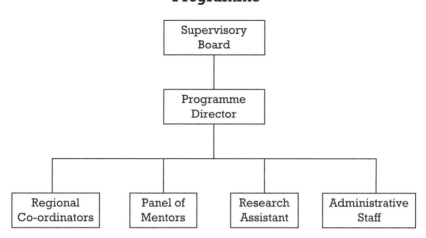

The panel of mentors can be divided into sub-panels of specialists in various fields of management — for example, general management, production, marketing, selling, IT, finance and engineering, to mention a few possibilities.

Supervisory Board

To start with, a supervisory board is appointed to agree the objectives of the programme and oversee their achievement. They will also supervise the progress of the development of the programme and ratify, or otherwise, proposals advanced by the programme director.

The supervisory board will comprise people who are representative of the various interests involved in the programme — for example, the promoters, the mentorees, the mentors, and business people with commercial experience and proven managerial expertise. Some of the board members should be high-profile business people to lend credibility to the programme.

Programme Director

The programme requires that one person be responsible for the orderly management of the programme. The person appointed to the position of programme director will have a good knowledge of best business practice, experience of management at a senior level, good human relations ability, knowledge of training practices and an understanding of the needs of the proprietors and managers of SMEs.

In the initial setting-up of the programme, the programme director will have to perform all the duties necessary to establish a viable, albeit small, mentor programme.

The programme director should establish and maintain contact with other mentor programmes as well as relevant business organisations at home and abroad.

The programme director should be aware of developments in business that could impact on mentorees and ensure that the mentors are briefed so that they will be able to discuss them with the mentorees. Particularly relevant are developments in IT and their impact on the channels of communication.

It is important that the programme director organise the initial briefing sessions for the programme co-ordinators and mentors. He will recognise, right from the beginning of the programme, that the transition from the role of manager or boss to that of mentor may not be easy for some of the new mentors on the programme. The training of mentors is discussed in *Chapter 8*.

With the growth of the programme, it will be necessary for the programme director to appoint regional co-ordinators and, if financially feasible, a research assistant.

Programme Co-ordinators

The function of the programme co-ordinators is to assist the programme director in the management of the mentors' assignments. They will maintain regular communication with the programme administration and with the mentorees and mentors during assignments.

The programme co-ordinators will be appointed on the basis of their proven management skills and the suitability of their location with reference to the area covered by the mentor programme. Their duties will include:

- Allocation of assignments to individual mentors

- Informing the mentorees what to expect from a mentoring assignment

- Examination of the mentors' reports

- Preparation of assessments of mentoring assignments, after interim and final consultation with the mentorees and mentors and consideration of the mentors' reports.

The allocation of the assignments will be made, as mentioned in the case of the programme director, on the basis of convenience of locations of the mentor and mentoree and the particular skill(s) required.

The programme co-ordinator must allow the mentor to exercise independence of thought, judgement and action, if the mentor is to perform his function effectively.

The programme co-ordinators must have online real-time access to the databases maintained by the programme office.

From the experience gained over time, the programme co-ordinators should be able to make recommendations for the improvement of the mentors' approaches to assignments and the continuing development of the programme.

Programme Co-ordinators' Meetings

The programme co-ordinators will attend group meetings called by the programme director. These meetings will alternate between meetings for co-ordinators only and meetings of co-ordinators and mentors.

On occasion, some mentorees should be invited to the joint meetings to give their assessment of an assignment that they have experienced. Opinions differ about the frequency of the meetings; some say every two months, others every three months. The spacing of the meetings is decided by the programme director as a compromise between the inconvenience of travelling and the necessity for regular face-to-face communication.

The agenda for the meetings will vary, depending on any specific issues arising in the progress of the programme but will usually include:

- A statement of the objectives of the meeting
- The programme director's report
- A statistical report on the progress of the programme
- Reports from the programme co-ordinators
- Any administrative issues
- A list of new mentors and their regional locations
- The reading of a short paper by an invited speaker on a topic relevant to the mentor programme
- A discussion of the paper
- Case studies by experienced mentors
- A review of the achievements of the meeting
- Suggested improvements for the next meeting
- Date of next meeting.

Time will be allowed for questions.

The provision of time for the co-ordinators and mentors to socialise, with a view to the exchange of information and ideas relevant to the programme, is usually welcome.

Programme Co-ordinator's Reports

Programme co-ordinators should submit a report to the programme director every month. The report will include statistics on:

- Assignments allocated to the region during the month
- Assignments completed during the past month
- Assignments in progress
- Mentoring assignment assessments
- Mentors available for assignments
- Mentors involved in assignments
- Mentorees on the waiting list for mentoring assignments.

A section of the report should be allocated for suggestions by the co-ordinator.

The programme co-ordinators' reports are logged into the database.

Research Assistant

To assist the continuous improvement and development of the mentor programme, it is advisable to appoint a research assistant. The primary task of the research assistant is to be a provider and source of information, including compiling all relevant statistics for the programme.

A review of the needs of the small and medium-sized enterprises in the area or industrial sectors served by the programme is the most likely starting point for research. This will require contact with participating mentorees and with SMEs that have not sought inclusion in the programme because of lack of awareness of its existence or lack of appreciation of its relevance to their organisation.

One analysis set will include the number, size and stated needs of the mentoree enterprises in the programme. Another will record the responses of the mentors to the stated needs of the mentorees and the related perceptions of the mentorees to these responses. These analyses will help to identify any shortcomings in the programme and/or mentors' approaches to assignments.

There will also be an analysis of the mentors' assessments of the programme seminars and briefings.

The research assistant, on the basis of business management trends and the statistics he has collected, can recommend to the programme director topics that will be of importance to mentorees and mentors.

From the reports of the research assistant will emerge suggestions for subjects to be discussed and classifications of case studies to be presented at the mentor briefings. They will also give pointers for topics in the mentor training/induction courses.

The research assistant will also identify sources of information on funding, grants and other assistance available to SMEs and maintain a library thereof.

Newsletter

Another useful means of maintaining communication with, and between, programme co-ordinators and mentors and, perhaps, mentorees is the issue of a newsletter by the programme director. This may be printed or displayed on the Internet or both.

It is probably advisable to outsource the editing of the newsletter, as it is probable that the publication would not justify a full-time professional editor and the finances of most mentor programmes are unlikely to be sufficient for such a luxury.

The editorial content of the newsletter will normally include:

- Mission statement of the programme

- Editorial

- Overview of progress of the mentor programme

- Satisfaction ratings of mentorees and mentors

- Topics arising from assignments

- Economic comment

- Administration news

- Staffing matters

- New mentors

- Diary of briefing sessions

- Case studies

- Statistics about number of assignments, number of mentors, geographical spread of mentor assignments, etc.

Frequency of publication has to be considered carefully as mentors and other potential readers are inundated with published material from solicited as well as unsolicited sources.

ADMINISTRATIVE SYSTEM

It is the responsibility of the programme director to create an administration system that, as well as maintaining the requisite financial records, statistical records, promotional material, correspondence files (hard copy or electronic) and channels of communication, will include a database of mentors and mentorees.

It will be necessary for the programme director to design formats for:

- The mentor *curriculum vitae* form

- The mentoree application form

- The mentors' report

- The mentors' expenses claims form

- The programme co-ordinators' report

- The programme co-ordinators' expenses claims form

- The assignment assessments form.

The programme director's staff will keep records and statistics of:

- The assignments allocated

- The current status of the assignments in progress

- The completion of the assignments

- The results of the assignments from the viewpoints of the mentors and the mentorees.

Administrative Staff

The function of the administrative staff is to support all the activities of the mentor programme. It will be necessary to recruit staff skilled in the various systems operated in the office. In addition, a training programme should be drafted to ensure the maintenance of their existing skills and their continuous improvement, and the acquisition of relevant new skills.

Staff must be provided with sufficient relevant information to work at optimum productivity. Furthermore, the work environment must be conducive to engendering enthusiasm for the job. "Work environment" includes salary, incentives, working conditions, employee empowerment, etc.

Regular staff meetings should be held to inform them of the latest developments in the programme and the impact of any changes in the administration function. It is important to explain and to demonstrate to the administration staff (with charts, if necessary — see *Figure 7.2*) the linkage of their work to the successful fulfilment of each aspect of the mentor programme.

Figure 7.2: How the Administrative Work Environment Contributes to Mentoree Satisfaction

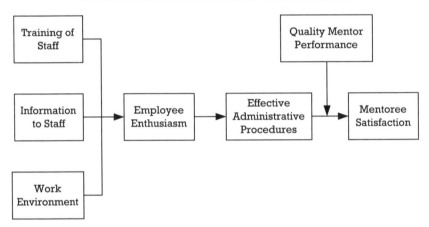

As well as the normal duties of typing letters, dealing with the incoming and outgoing post, filing, reception and telephone answering, the administrative staff issue application forms to potential mentors and mentorees and maintain and update the database of mentors and mentorees. They also supply the regional co-ordinators with copies of the mentors' reports.

As stated previously, the accounting function is a part of the administrative responsibility.

The administration staff validate the payment claims from co-ordinators and mentors and invoices from commercial creditors and process payments to them.

PANEL OF MENTORS

Having established an administrative system, the next function of the programme director is to appoint a panel of mentors. The members of the supervisory board may be able to assist him in this task. *Chapter 8* on the selection and training of mentors will be of assistance here.

Appointment of Mentors

An application to join the panel of mentors should be accompanied by a recommendation from the promoters, a supervisor, an active mentor, a programme co-ordinator or a business entrepreneur known to the programme director. This subject is dealt with in detail in *Chapter 8*.

Having received the application, the programme director will meet the applicant and, if he is considered suitable, will invite him to an introductory meeting of prospective new mentors. If the applicant confirms his wish to join the mentor panel after attendance at the introductory meeting, the programme director will send the new mentor a letter of acceptance onto the mentor panel together with a copy of the mentor manual (see below).

The prospective new mentor is then invited to the next training/induction meeting for mentors. Some programme co-ordinators will attend these meetings.

The agenda for the introductory meeting will include:

- A statement of the objectives of the meeting

- Introduction to the history, objectives, structure and progress of the programme by the programme director

- Presentation of the mentor manual by a programme co-ordinator

- Review of a few mentor case studies by experienced mentors

- Explanation of the administrative procedures by an administrative assistant

- Questions and answers

- Achievements of the meeting
- Suggested improvements for future induction meetings.

Specialist Panels

The programme director may deem it helpful to establish specialist panels of mentors to advise on such matters as start-up, general management, production processes, marketing, selling, IT, finance, engineering, and business excellence, to mention a few possibilities. There may also be specialist panels of mentors with experience in particular industries.

A mentor engaged on an assignment may identify the need for a specialist mentor and apply to the programme director for one to be appointed. The specialist mentor will co-ordinate with the mentor in charge of the assignment.

Mentor Briefings

The mentors will attend briefing meetings every three months to appraise them of developments in the programme, to review case studies and to network with other mentors and administrative staff.

The agenda for these briefing meetings will include:

- A statement of the objectives of the meeting
- New initiatives in the programme
- Information about matters affecting SMEs
- Review of a few case studies by experienced mentors
- A paper read by a guest speaker on a subject relevant to the mentor programme
- Questions and answers
- Achievements of the meeting
- Suggested improvements for future mentor meetings.

The Mentor's Reports

The mentor's reports are directly related to the objectives of the assignment. The objectives are usually articulated in the letter of appointment to the mentor. On occasion, the objectives are modified after the mentor has conducted an initial assessment of the mentoree's needs. Any such changes should only be undertaken after agreement with the programme director and the mentoree.

As the assignment is likely to extend over many months, the mentor will be expected to submit interim reports to the programme director, after every two or three visits to the entrepreneur. These reports need not be too lengthy. It is sufficient for the mentor to indicate how the objectives are being tackled and how close to their achievement the assignment has progressed.

The mentor's final report restates the objectives of the assignment and whether they have been achieved in whole or part. Where the objectives have proved to be too ambitious for the time period allocated to the assignment, this should be stated with a recommendation for appropriate further action. The recommendation may be that some time should be allowed for the company to absorb whatever changes were wrought during the assignment. On the other hand, it might be recommended that an additional assignment be granted to the mentoree for the same mentor or another mentor with a more appropriate skill.

Where the mentor's out-of-pocket expenses, such as travelling, telephone or stationery, are allowed for reimbursement, the mentor should be encouraged to submit his expense claims when sending in his reports. This practice makes the administrative work expeditious and more controllable.

Mentor Manual

The drafting of a Mentor Manual for distribution to the mentors is another responsibility of the programme director.

The manual will include:

- A description of the mentor programme, and its objectives

- The structure and staffing of the programme

- Guidelines for mentors

- Examples of the reports required and requirements for their submission

- Instructions for submission of expenses

- Confidentiality Agreement

- Background material for participating enterprises

- Code of Conduct for mentors.

Code of Conduct

The programme director should also, as part of the setting-up tasks, draft a Code of Conduct for mentors. A model is included in the *Appendix*.

ATTRACTION OF MENTOREES

Once the systems are in place and functioning, the next step is to generate applications for mentors from the proprietors and managers of small and medium-sized enterprises.

These applicants will be screened to ascertain the enterprises' needs and their abilities to benefit from the services of a mentor or mentors.

MENTORING ASSIGNMENTS

The allocation of the mentor assignments to the mentors comes next. This will involve consideration of the geographical locations of the mentorees, the available mentors in that location and the particular skills required for the assignment, as perceived by the mentoree and the programme director. In due time, the mentor will form his own perception of the mentoree's needs.

The matching of the mentoree with the mentor is the key to the success of the programme.

Assessment of Assignments

Assessment of assignment reports must be submitted to the programme director by the programme co-ordinators. These reports will be presented on completion of an assignment and following consideration of the mentor's final report and a final debriefing of the mentoree.

The main focus of this report is the comparison of the objectives of the assignment and the results achieved. The assessment report is not restricted to the opinion of the mentoree but also records the mentor's viewpoint. This topic is dealt with in more detail in *Chapter 9*.

FINANCE

The mentor programme has to be financed, in order to pay set-up and day-to-day running costs. It goes without saying that capital and revenue budgets should be prepared in consultation with the staff who will be responsible for the management of activities covered by the budget. All participants in the programme should be notified of the sections of the budget relevant to their work.

Set-up costs arise from:

- The expense of acquiring an office lease
- Decoration of the office
- Office furniture
- IT equipment
- Software
- Photocopiers
- Scanners
- Dictating equipment
- Filing facilities
- Telephones
- The usual small office tools such as staplers, binding machines and paper-punchers.

Day-to-day expenses include:

- Salaries

- Social insurance costs and other benefits

- Regional co-ordinators' and mentors' honorariums

- Rent and services

- Communication costs such as telephone, fax, e-mail, stationery, including the various forms, and postage

- Printing of the programme brochure

- Printing of the annual report

- Printing of the mentor manual

- IT costs

- Light and heat

- Travelling costs

- Staff training costs

- Entertainment.

If the programme engages in promotion of its services, marketing costs will be incurred. These will include promotional material, advertising and the cost of channels of communication, both personalised and non-personalised.

The training of programme co-ordinators and mentors, as well as administrative personnel, will also involve costs. These costs will include rent of the training location, fees to the trainer, rent of equipment, printing of the documentation handouts, meals and, possibly, the cost of transport to and from the training location.

The cost of the induction meetings, the training sessions for new mentors and the regular meetings of co-ordinators and mentors will have to be provided for, too. There may be speakers' fees, if papers are presented at these meetings. The costs of these meetings will be similar to the costs of the training meetings listed above.

SELECTION AND TRAINING OF A MENTOR

SELECTION

The selection of a person to become a mentor is as complex an activity as any recruitment process in business, because there are as many questions to be answered in mentor recruitment as there are in any employment interview.

Mentor's Age

To take but one example: how relevant is the age of the applicant? Obviously, it has some relevance because, as a minimum, a person needs time to gain experience of business, and of life to acquire humility. One is unlikely to garner sufficient management experience to be a mentor in, say, less than ten years. Apart from the time required to have gained and stored sufficient experience to be a mentor, the age profile of prospective mentorees has to be taken into account. A difference in age of a generation between mentor and mentoree may be too great. If the mentoree is given a choice to pick a mentor from a shortlist of three, as he should, it gives him the opportunity to decide on the question of age, among other factors.

Business people in their 30s and 40s tend to be concentrating on growing their businesses or building their careers. In their 50s, it is not uncommon for them to look around for a new challenge. Mentoring could provide that challenge.

Headhunting

In starting a mentoring programme, it is better to headhunt suitable candidates for the mentor panel. Their track record suggests to the programme director their suitability. Unfamiliar applicants require exhaustive investigation and can take up scarce time.

Mentor's Appearance

The suitability of the mentor's appearance, clothes, attitude and general tidiness is a matter of opinion on which the director of the mentor programme must decide since he knows the clientele. Certain minimum standards should be expected. Many mentors are retired from full-time occupation and, perhaps, adopt a more relaxed approach to sartorial standards. The criterion is the likely initial impression that will be made on the mentoree. There is no doubt that, ultimately, the contribution the mentor makes to the mentoree's business will be what is assessed, not his appearance. Behaviour, knowledge and skills that are admired will overcome many perceived shortcomings.

Reasons for Becoming a Mentor

A key question to ask the aspiring mentor is what he expects or wishes to derive from the mentoring experience; for example:

- Does he wish to give something back to society?

- Does he, possibly a retired person, wish "to keep his hand in"?

- Does the potential mentor have an awareness of his own strengths and weaknesses?

- Is the prospective mentor prepared to be a sounding board?

- Is he interested in the continuing use of feedback as a measurement of progress?

Nothing could be worse than to engage someone who has time on his hands and is looking for a pastime to fill it. Most businesspeople who become mentors have a genuine desire to pass on the fruits of their own experience in the hope that it will be of help to others. They are conscious of what they themselves missed when they could have done with a mentor and none was available.

Mentor's Experience

The experience of a potential mentor is of critical importance. Mentors are often classified by the nature of their qualifications and the skills they have practised during their careers to date. They may have specialised in a particular activity or have taken the route of general management. As Henri Fayol (1841–1925) pointed out in his seminal book *General and Industrial Management*, managers quite often start their careers in business with a specialist skill, be it engineering, chemical, financial or accounting, which they practise for several years before later progressing into general management.

Level of Management Experience

Previously we stated that experience of business at a senior level is essential. The knowledge of the processes involved in making decisions is the raw material with which the mentor works. Manifest confidence derived from the practice of management over a long period is a quality admired by most mentorees.

The hierarchical level of the current business occupation or former occupation of the proposed mentor can have a fundamental bearing on the suitability of an aspiring mentor. To achieve the management status occupied, very likely he worked his way up the organisation from a junior level. Provided there has not been too long a time lapse between the junior status and the senior position, the mentor applicant will remember the nature of the challenges faced by sections of departments in a business. In many ways, these challenges are similar to those faced by small business. The difference is, of course, that the small unit in the larger enterprise is able to call on significant resources to overcome difficulties encountered in achieving their goals. Furthermore, they are, to some extent, insulated from the adverse consequences of poor decisions.

The small independent firm does not have similar resources to tap into or that protection from the detrimental outcome of faulty judgement. The limitations of a small firm's ability to overcome an obstacle to its commercial progress needs to be recognised by the mentor. Gone are the halcyon days of summoning a department head to delegate to him a task or project or to seek an answer for his failure to attain a target set for him. In a small enterprise, the person sitting in front of the mentor is most likely the combined production manager, sales manager, chief accountant, personnel manager, the research chemist and who knows what else.

When we refer to business experience, experience gained in a non-profit-making enterprise is not excluded. The same management principles are applied in both types of organisation.

Mentor's Current Activity

The current activity of the prospective mentor has a bearing on his suitability. A person who is in the throes of a major reorganisation of his own business will hardly have available time to devote to the problems of a mentoree. It may seem strange but, sometimes, a person feels impelled to allocate time to helping others even though they are facing a crisis in their own business or personal life. The programme director will probably feel that it is more productive for such a person to sort out their current problems before embarking on mentor assignments.

Being engaged in a business or a profession at the time of interview does not make the applicant ineligible to be a mentor. In many cases, their occupation is particularly suitable for inclusion in the mentor programme. It is, largely, a question of the extent of their involvement. And they have one advantage to contribute to the mentor programme, the benefit of being "in the thick of things".

Retired Businesspeople

The vocation of mentor seems especially appropriate for retired businesspeople. They are presumed to have the requisite free time to dedicate to the mentoree and, assuming pertinent experience and attitude, their contribution can be invaluable.

It is accepted that their focus will have changed or will change as their new status of retired person impacts on them. But this can be advantageous for the mentoree, as the mentor will find it easier to consider issues in a more detached manner, free from any personal business pressures.

It is unlikely that the retired person will view the function of mentor simply as an activity to pass the time, because of the mentoree's expectation that the mentor will contribute to the development of his business.

Characteristics of a Mentor

The person selecting a mentor should look for the ability to analyse a case or problem, and then to present it to a mentoree in the form of question and answer — and then to guide the mentoree to suggest options, using the same method of applying the question-and-answer format (the Socratic method explained earlier). This type of presentation, which can be verbal or electronic or a combination of both, is the basis of mentoring.

It is difficult to see how a mentor can function without having significant interpersonal skills. The capacity to relate to people in a non-confrontational manner and without over-ebullience is essential. It is part of the gift of communicating. The mentor must be able to express encouragement and support in a manner that the mentoree finds acceptable. Refer to *Chapter 2* for a more detailed look at characteristics of a mentor.

Transformation from Boss to Mentor

The competence to deal with this change in circumstance is what is required from a former chief executive when he becomes a mentor. It is not an easy transformation. Can he cross that divide? The programme director must decide.

The mentoree would like his relatively modest status to be appreciated by the mentor, although that very standing may be the starting point for what could be seen as over-ambitious goals. The businessperson who has kept in touch with small firms has a better chance of meeting the criteria set by the interviewing programme director. At the same time, the director will recruit only those who are adaptable and sufficiently versatile to see the big picture as well as being capable of working in a small scenario.

Less than Omniscient

The mentor function does not confer infallibility or omniscience. The prospective mentor needs to appreciate that fact. The mentor is at pains to impress on the mentoree that the process is a joint one, an exchange of ideas, hopefully fruitful ones.

Time Available

A key factor in the selection of a mentor is the time that the mentor not only has available, but is prepared to spend on mentoring assignments. The time commitment varies from assignment to assignment and can be inconvenient at times, clashing as it will with other activities. That is the nature of a mentor's undertaking and the programme director will need to look for flexibility here.

TRAINING

Having selected a mentor panel, what training, if any, do they need to become effective mentors? Is training even the right word?

The mentors have been selected on the basis of their experience and suitability for the programme. Can they be given an assignment right away, without more ado? Perhaps not. There are many topics of importance to the efficient and effective process of mentoring that may not have featured in the career of each new mentor. Orientation or briefing sessions may be more appropriate than a formal training course.

The dramatic change from being a boss, at some management level, who is used to directing, to being a mentor, who must exercise unending patience in guiding a mentoree to consider various options available to him, can be traumatic. This necessary, if not entirely obvious, change lies at the heart of the transition from management executive to mentor. It forms the core subject of any mentor training course, orientation or briefing session.

The new attributes to be inculcated are:

- The need to listen rather than talk may be the most difficult transformation asked of the new mentor. As boss, he was accustomed to doing the talking. He must now change to become a listener. We have referred to the requirement for listening skills right through this book and a presentation in depth of the art of listening should be the first topic in the induction session.

- The management executive is used to issuing instructions about how things are to be done or not done. A completely different attitude is now demanded by his new status. His new approach as mentor is to *ask* why something is done or not done. He may then, if he deems it appropriate, challenge the mentoree to explore other possibilities and, perhaps, ask him to suggest additional options, thus testing the mentoree's presumptions and conviction about the *status quo*.

- In **Chapter 6**, we referred to the need for the mentoree to work *on* the business as distinct from working *in* the business. The changed approach for the new mentor requires him to work *with* the mentoree as he (the mentoree) works *on* the business.

- The boss is in control. The mentor does not control. The mentoree controls his business. The new mentor must accept and retain these relationships always clearly in his mind. The mentor looks for the mentoree's commitment to the mentoring process. He must never seek to exercise any control in the mentoree's business.

- The management executive does not necessarily establish friendly relationships with his staff. That is not to say that they are unfriendly; civility rather than friendliness is the rule. The mentor seeks to be the mentoree's business friend.

The mentor training programme has as its objective the transformation of a boss, manager, management executive, into a mentor, a guide.

The differences in the roles are many.

Figure 8.1: Boss and Mentor Contrasted

The Boss . . .	The Mentor . . .
Talks	Listens
Tells	Asks questions
Works **on** the business	Works **with** the business
Controls	Seeks commitment
Sets objectives	Seeks objectives
Sets goals	Challenges goals
Asks "Did you do that?"	Asks "Have you thought of?"
Asks "When will it be done?"	Asks "What resources have you?"
Instructs	Guides
Assesses	Explores
Takes	Gives
Has a short-time frame	Is future-orientated
Wants a quick fix	Seeks preventive measures
Focuses on the bottom line	Focuses on the processes
Blames	Seeks improvement
Is aloof	Is accessible/friendly
Obtains information giving power	Shares knowledge
Has experience of big business	Works with small and medium-sized firms

Programme Objectives

The organisers of the mentor programme will have drafted the objectives of the programme. These objectives are among the first facts to be communicated to the new mentors, informing them of the corporate purpose of the programme and the parameters within which the mentors will operate.

Mentoree's Objectives

As the mentoree is the focus of every assignment, his needs and aspirations will be the subject of considerable discussion. This is only as it should be.

Mentors have their own views but it is the mentoree's opinion that holds sway, at least in the initial stages of the assignment. What happens afterwards depends on the progress the mentor and mentoree make together.

Mentor's Objectives

A new mentor is keen to know what is expected of him in conducting a mentoring assignment and, unfortunately, it is not easy to set invariable standards for him to achieve in every case he is allotted. Each assignment is different in its circumstances and the aspirations of the entrepreneur to be mentored. This lack of consistency or wished-for conformity is another subject for debate in the induction briefing.

No mentor briefing session would be complete without a frank examination of the aspirations of the mentors participating in the programme. Encouraging debate among the mentors may be the best approach to this subject. The assistance of an experienced facilitator in these discussions is usually helpful, not only in providing shape to the exchanges but also in arriving at conclusions.

Mentoring Assessments

Inevitably, the topics of success and failure in assignments, and what goes between, are raised. It is good that they are. Better to realise at the beginning that not all assignments end in success, however defined, than to face baffled incomprehension when confronted with a job that just hasn't worked or, more often, hasn't progressed as well as expected.

Case Studies

Taking into consideration both the business experience of the new mentors and their lack of mentoring experience, one of the most valuable parts of the induction briefing is the provision of case studies prepared by practising mentors. These can be very illuminating in their description of the various situations mentors have found themselves, not all of them as rewarding as might be expected. Prospective mentors can hear about mentorees' problems and how the mentor and mentoree sought their resolution. It is, also, a further opportunity for the new recruits to hear about perceived successes and failures and how these were handled.

Mentor Briefings

The frequency of briefings depends on the needs of the people appointed — their needs as defined by the mentors themselves as much as their needs as perceived by the administration.

In any event, it is beneficial to have several briefings every year to bring the mentors up-to-date on developments within the programme. It is also salutary to bring the mentors together regularly to exchange notes and to hear more case studies.

Special Topics

Although the mentors have perhaps two or more decades of experience, there are bound to be special topics that are relevant to them in their function as mentors. These have arisen currently, such as new government regulations, additions to the range of financial products available, government grant assistance or developments in technology with which they may not be familiar. The presenters at these briefings will, generally, come from organisations that specialise in these topics.

Mentors who provide specialist skill mentoring are expected to keep up-to-date themselves in their own field, as it would not be realistic for the programme organisers to take responsibility for that kind of updating.

Mentor's Methodology

The methodology to be used by mentors in their periodic meetings with the mentorees can be left to the mentors, if that is what they wish. Many mentors develop their own techniques that serve them well. Some mentors may ask for guidance from the mentor organisation about proven methodology in conducting mentoring dialogue.

An example of a successful methodology can be found in the *Plato Dialogues* in which Socrates is the main problem-solver. Socrates could be described as the greatest mentor of all time. His method of seeking solutions with his interrogators was to ask questions. The method is best exemplified in the dialogue *Meno*, referred to earlier. It contains a master lesson on the search for answers by asking questions. At no stage does Socrates suggest a solution to a problem. By asking questions, he proceeds with the mentoree inexorably towards the sought-for answer.

Administration

There are many bureaucratic procedures to be observed in an organisation or programme and these will be introduced to the new mentors at the induction sessions. These usually take the form of documentation that must be completed by the mentor during the course of a mentoring assignment. These documents are used to monitor the progress of the assignment and are essential to the orderly management of the programme.

Mentor Training Sessions

An outline for a series of eight mentor training sessions is shown in *Figure 8.2*.

Figure 8.2: Mentor Training Sessions

Session 1
Statement of objective of
session.
Welcome to Mentor
Programme.
What is Mentoring
Mentoring through the Ages

Session 5
Statement of objective of
session.
The transition from Boss to
Mentor.
Case Study.

Session 2
Statement of objective of the
session.
Mentor Programme Objectives.
Mentoree's Objectives.
Mentor's Objectives.
Congruence of Objectives.

Session 6
Statement of objective of
session.
Code of Conduct.
Case Study.

Session 3
Statement of objective of
session.
Characteristics of a Mentor.
Characteristics of a Mentoree.
What a Mentoree expects from
a Mentor.
What a Mentor expects from a
Mentoree.
Congruence of characteristics
and expectations.

Session 7
Statement of objective of
session.
Mentor Self-Assessment.
Programme Assessment of
Mentoring Assignment.
Assessment Questionnaire.
Case Study.

Session 4
Statement of objective of
session.
The Art of Listening.
The Listening Mentoree.
Illustration of Socratic Dialogue

Session 8
Statement of objective of
session.
Programme Administration
Requirements.
Schedule of Mentor Briefing
sessions during next twelve
months.
Case Study.

ASSESSMENT OF MENTOR ASSIGNMENTS

EVALUATION

A proper assessment of a mentor assignment at its conclusion is essential for the continuous improvement of a Mentor Programme. The evaluation of the assignment, obviously, includes an appraisal of the mentor's contribution to the process.

Uniqueness of Business Entity

In assessing the assignment, it is relevant to recognise at the outset that each business entity is unique, with its own history, culture, capabilities, resources and strategic vision. It is pertinent to note, also, that the industry in which each enterprise operates has its own particular circumstances and critical success factors. The enterprise's position in its industry and that industry's vogue in terms of appeal and profitability is another determinant. And the economic climate of the period during which an assignment is carried out must be taken into account, because economic environments change. How the mentor takes these elements into account and his ability to communicate his sensitivity to these issues is important.

Assessment Criteria

To the detached observer, a comparison of the enterprise's position at the beginning of the assignment with the position at the end might seem to be the only criteria of merit — that is, until one tries to define either position, apart altogether from assessing them. There are more factors to be considered than profit, sales, employment, etc.

The more difficult cases are those in which the mentoree confesses to having lost his sense of direction and feels isolated, lacking someone knowledgeable to talk to in confidence. In that type of assignment, the quality of the mentor/mentoree relationship is of paramount importance. The mentoree's readiness to unburden himself to the mentor is inspired by his perception of their mutual compatibility. And their ability to communicate with one another is a large factor in establishing their level of compatibility. It can be said that, if they cannot communicate intelligibly, compatibility is practically impossible. How is the application of these concepts measured? Certainly not by profit pre- and post-assignment.

We should bear in mind that some mentorees are more capable than others at evaluating in an objective and analytical manner the actual achievements of an assignment. For that reason, the trend of a mentor's scores in his assignments and the average score over a period may be more informative than the score from any individual assignment.

In some cases — those of a specialist nature, whether functional or industrial — the mentoree identifies a problem and seeks a mentor from a specialist panel to assist in finding a solution. If the problem is solved or the circumstances are ameliorated to some extent, the assessment of that assignment is relatively straightforward (or so it would appear), although the level of success has still to be adjudicated.

Where the assignment is a limited one dealing with marketing, production, personnel, administration or financial matters, for example, the assessment of the assignment must still take into account the level of strategic planning involved and the contribution of the mentor to its accomplishment. For these reasons, the assessment of a mentor assignment is complex.

Other Criteria

Although the mentoree is the recipient of the mentoring and, in that sense, can be regarded as the customer, his opinion, while of the utmost importance, is not the only criterion. If the mentoree is pleased with the process and believes that he has gained from it, then the assignment has been successful, from his point of view.

But to leave it at that would be inadvisable. That is not to say that customer satisfaction is not paramount but, as stated previously, other factors must be considered. As in any enterprise, the pursuit of excellence includes:

- Continuous assessment of customer needs

- Satisfying those needs

- Consistent improvement of the service provided

- The development of further services beneficial to the customer.

So it is with a Mentor Programme. On the one hand, there is the mentoree's perception of the effectiveness or success of the process and, on the other hand, the relationship of that perception to the actual achievements of the mentor assignment. In **Chapter 6**, we mentioned the "window test" and its relevance to evaluations of communication and understanding.

The assessment is based on the assumption that both the mentor and the mentoree were seeing the same industry, the same organisation, the same business activity, the same products, but perhaps not the same current circumstance nor the same potential.

ASSESSMENT QUESTIONNAIRE

The goal of this chapter is to articulate a method of assessment and to design the format of a mentor assignment evaluation report (see the end of this chapter). The problem is the question or questions to be asked. We will propose the content of a questionnaire. We have tried to keep the questionnaire as short as possible while, at the same time, asking a sufficient number of questions to yield a fair appreciation of the assignment's value.

The mentoree, the mentor and the programme director (or regional co-ordinator, as appropriate) ideally reach a consensus about the success or otherwise of the assignment, its merits or demerits. The mentoree may view the process in terms of success or failure and the mentor may judge it in terms of effectiveness within the entity's unique set of circumstances. Nonetheless, already we have identified two yardsticks that should feature in an evaluation:

- Communication

- The mentor's awareness of the business and its industry.

Where the mentor and mentoree differ about the potential of the business, it is the mentoree's vision that prevails because it his business and the decisions are his. This consideration, then, does not appear on the assessment form.

Assessment

The assessment form comprises a questionnaire with a columnar points section. The opinions of the mentor and mentoree are recorded on this document by means of points awarded in response to their answers to the statements listed on the questionnaire.

The programme director asks the questions and completes the form. After completing the questionnaire with the mentoree, he then goes through the same questionnaire with the mentor using the same wording.

The use of the same format for both mentoree and mentor makes it much easier to compare their views of the progress of the assignment. It may also give some inkling of the level of compatibility of the participants.

The Questions

The topics to be evaluated and the statements to do so are set out below.

1. The mentor needs to have an appreciation of the industry in which the mentoree operates. **Statement:** *The mentor was able to relate easily to our industry.*

2. The mentor needs to have developed an appreciation of the mentoree's business. **Statement:** *The mentor understood my business.*

3. We have emphasised the importance of agreeing the objectives of the mentoring assignment at the beginning, perhaps not on the first encounter but as soon as possible thereafter. Any vagueness about this element of mentoring is noteworthy and should be part of the assessment. **Statement:** *The mentor and I agreed the objectives of the assignment.*

4. The mentoree will have undertaken several tasks during the mentor assignment with target completion dates. **Statement:** *The mentor and I agreed the tasks to be completed by me and their target dates so that the objectives of the assignment could be achieved.*

5. In some of these, the mentor will have guided the mentoree towards a possible achievement. The nature and extent of the guidance and the clarity of communication will determine the quality of the fulfilment. **Statement:** *The mentor gave clear guidance on the process of achievement of the objectives.*

6. Assuming that the objectives of the assignment were agreed at or close to the start, it is pertinent to know whether the tasks identified were completed on time. An easily identifiable measurement is the number of declared tasks that were completed on time. Both mentor and mentoree will have their own ideas about the level of achievement and the process of arriving at it. **Statement:** *I completed on time all the tasks agreed with the mentor.*

7. The ability of the mentor to communicate is of paramount importance. Clarity of expression, patience, accessibility, listening are components of communication. **Statement:** *The mentor communicated clearly and was easy to relate to.*

8. The exchange of ideas — mentor to mentoree, mentoree to mentor — is a fundamental feature of mentoring. If the mentor supplied all the ideas, how is the mentoree to comment on the sharing of ideas? **Statement:** *The exchange of ideas between the mentor and me was useful.*

9. The passing on of information and skills is the core of mentoring. The mentor must be seen to have done so by the mentoree. **Statement:** *The mentor introduced me to several new ideas. (For example: structured meetings, strategic planning, marketing techniques, production planning, staff training, budgeting, cash flow management, costing, pricing, etc.)*

10. Without employing a psychiatrist to evaluate the level of compatibility, the best that can be done is to question the mentoree and the mentor about their perceptions of the level of compatibility and, indeed, their opinion of its relevance. Much depends on the mentor's approach and the mentoree's response to it. The progress of the process is largely dependent on how the relationship functions. This aspect provides a fundamental insight about the dynamics of the assignment. **Statement:** *The mentor and I got on well together.*

11. Was the mentor enthusiastic? This is an important question for the mentoree to answer. Obviously, enthusiasm alone could be nugatory. Focused enthusiasm is what is relevant. **Statement:** *The mentor brought enthusiasm to the assignment.*

12. The mentoree's enthusiasm is also relevant. This question supports or negates Question 10. **Statement:** *I was enthusiastic during the mentor assignment.*

13. The mentor may have quoted particular cases, relevant to the assignment on hand, or focused exclusively on general maxims. **Statement:** *The mentor quoted relevant cases experienced by him.*

14. Mentors must be competent not only as business people but also as mentors. Incompetence, or something less than competence, is often a matter of opinion but the question must be asked. What appears to be incompetent in one example may be an Homeric nod not repeated by the mentor in other assignments. The mentor's opinion may differ and, of course, he will make that clear in the assessment form. **Statement:** *The mentor was competent.*

15. The assignment should be characterised by discipline. This question refers to such criteria as punctuality, timeliness in delivery, focus on topics without distraction, seriousness, cut-off without tardiness, appreciation of one another's commitment to others, and follow through. Dedication to the assignment by both parties is essential. Here again, we are dependent on the separate perceptions of this element of the mentoree and mentor. **Statement:** *The assignment was conducted in a timely and disciplined fashion.*

16. The foregoing might appear to exclude work enjoyment, but that is not the intention. As mentioned previously, a sense of humour is a great boon in business and also in mentoring. To enjoy the assignment is to make it more pleasant for everyone and aids the achievement of the as-signment's objectives. **Statement:** *The mentoring assign-ment was enjoyable.*

17. The pace of the mentor process will vary from assignment to assignment. The mentoree will, largely, dictate the pace. **Statement:** *The pace of the mentoring was appropriate.*

18. The mentoring assignment should be characterised by the achievement of the objectives that were agreed at the be-ginning. **Statement:** *The objectives agreed at the beginning were achieved.*

19. One long-term goal of the mentoring process, as has been said before, is that the mentoree might, in time, become a mentor. **Statement:** *I would be able to be a mentor.*

20. An essential feature of the mentoring process is the ability of both parties to disengage on completion of the assign-ment. **Statement:** *Disengagement was not difficult.*

21. It is useful to have a catch-all question that summarises the totality of the experience. **Statement:** *I would repeat the ex-perience.*

Scoring

The mentoree is asked to indicate his level of agreement with each of the above statements over a range:

- Agree Strongly

- Agree

- No Opinion

- Disagree

- Disagree Strongly

- Not Relevant.

The points awarded range from 5 for Agree Strongly to 1 for Disagree Strongly; 0 is recorded for Not Relevant.

Figure 9.1: Example

Please indicate your level of agreement with each of the following statements by putting an (X) in the appropriate space (ee = mentoree, or = mentor)

	Agree Strongly 5		Agree 4		No Opinion 3		Disagree 2		Disagree Strongly 1		Not Relevant 0	
	ee	or	ee	or	ee	or	ee	or	ee	or	ee	or
1. The mentor under-stood our industry												
2. The mentor under-stood my business												
3. The mentor and I agreed objectives												
....												

The conclusions are evaluated on a numerical scoring basis and compared (see *Figure 9.2*).

Figure 9.2: Example 2

Please indicate your level of agreement with each of the following statements by putting an (X) in the appropriate space (ee = mentoree, or = mentor)

	Agree Strongly 5		Agree 4		No Opinion 3		Disagree 2		Disagree Strongly 1		Not Relevant 0	
	ee	or	ee	or	ee	or	ee	or	ee	or	ee	or
………												
17. The pace was ideal			X	X								
18. I would be able to be a mentor				X	X							
19. Disengagement was not difficult	X			X								
20. I would repeat the experience			X			X						
Points Scored	5	0	8	12	3	3	0	0	0	0	0	0
Total Points Scored	16	15										
Maximum Points Possible (4 x 5)	20	20										
%	80	75										

The mentoree's rating of the assignment is equivalent to a customer's or a client's rating. The mentor's satisfaction rating is equivalent to a supplier's rating. If the mentoree's rating of the assignment and the mentor's rating are at odds with one another by ten per cent or more, further inquiry should be made to ascertain the reason for the disparity.

Not only can the assessment be evaluated discretely but the information on this form can also be combined with those of other assignments completed by the mentor to provide a trend or graph of customers' satisfaction with that mentor.

By combining the results of this assessment with all other assessments of the mentor panel, the overall mentoree satisfaction rating can be obtained.

Once again, trends can be plotted. Furthermore, assessments of individual topics can be combined to identify any subjects that are not achieving satisfactory ratings.

Therefore, we now have:

- The mentoree's assessment of the assignment

- The mentor's assessment of the assignment

- The individual mentor's rating trend in all his assignments to date, or for a defined period, awarded by mentorees, plotted on a trend sheet or graph to assess the level of satisfaction achieved

- The overall mentor's rating of assignments to date since commencement and for defined periods

- The overall rating of individual topics awarded by mentorees for each mentor, thereby indicating areas for improvement

- The overall rating of individual topics awarded by the mentor thereby indicating his/her identification of areas for self-improvement

- The overall rating of individual topics for the panel of mentors awarded by both mentors and mentorees. This measurement provides material for the briefing sessions of mentors.

From these, we can calculate indices of the progress of the mentor programme.

Mentors and the Assessment Form

The results of each assessment are of vital interest to the mentor and he/she should be informed of the outcome. Both the mentor and the programme director should meet periodically to discuss the trend of the evaluations of the mentor's assignments.

At the quarterly meetings of mentors, combined results of assessments of all mentors' assignments should be published.

We emphasise that the debriefing results — that is, the points awarded on the assessment form — are not to be presented in a critical or confrontational manner. To do so could lead to a diminution in the number of mentors available to the programme. The objective is continuous improvement of the mentoring process by identifying areas or topics needing enhancement.

Figure 9.3 gives an example of a script that a programme director might use in conducting the questionnaire with a mentoree. Clearly, the same process with the mentor, with whom he would be more familiar, would be less formal.

Figure 9.3: Mentor Assessment

Introduction

My name is .... I am calling you on behalf of the XYZ Mentoring Programme, for which I am the programme director.

The purpose of this call is to find out how well the mentoring assignment just finished has lived up to your expectations.

I do this after every mentoring assignment.

I am interested in your opinions about the mentoring that you have received. Your views will be helpful to me for the continuous improvement of the programme and its future development.

The assessment will take about X minutes.

I hope that you will agree to answer the small number of questions I have listed here.

Assessment of Mentoring Assignment

Mentor Name	
Job Reference	
Mentoree's Name	
Mentoree's Address	
Regional Co-ordinator	
Date Assignment Began	
Date Assignment Ended	
Date of Report	

Please rate the following by putting an (X) in the appropriate space (ee = mentoree, or = mentor):

	Very Useful 5		Useful 4		Of Some Use 3		No Opinion 2		Not Useful 1		Not Relevant 0	
	ee	or	ee	or	ee	or	ee	or	ee	or	ee	or
Statement 1												
Statement 2												
...												
...												
...												
...												
...												
...												
...												
...												
...												
...												
...												
...												
...												
...												
...												
...												
...												
...												
Statement 21												
Points Scored												
Total Points Scored												
Maximum Points Possible (x 5)												
%												

Entered in the Database: ....

Date:..............................

Figure 9.4 gives an example of a form that a prospective mentoree might complete to apply for a mentor to be assigned to him.

Figure 9.4: Application Form

Name of Applicant	
Address of Applicant	

Telephone:	Mobile:
E-mail:	Fax:

Promoters	
Nature of business	
Main products	
Is business plan available?	

Objectives in applying for mentor	
Mentor experience/skill required	

Business background	
Date trading commenced	
Type of legal entity	
Approximate turnover	
Approximate profit	
Management accounts available?	
Date of last audit	
Number of staff	

Mentoree's Objectives

10

QUO VADIS MENTORING?

It is a truism to say that, as business changes, mentoring will change. One would need to be a modern day seer to state categorically how business will change. The only thing one can be sure of is that it *will* change; it has done so since the inception of commerce. We see it today with the information technology explosion. The same applies to business processes, be they production, marketing or administrative. The response in the mentoring function will be equally dramatic. It will manifest itself in developed forms of communication, advanced technological skills, and heightened human relations ability.

CHANGES IN THE BUSINESS ENVIRONMENT

The business environment is also changing. Business ethics is a subject at the forefront of people's concerns. The effects of business on the natural ecology are a world problem. Fairness in the workplace is receiving far more public attention. Discussion of business processes in a mentoring assignment takes account of these matters, both as a matter of course and by choice, but in the future it will be obligatory to do so.

Size of Business

Mentors deal with, in the main, small and medium-sized businesses. Staff levels, even in these firms, are likely to decrease with the introduction of more technology in the various processes of commercial activity. This does not mean that personnel management will not be as important. It is likely that it will assume greater importance. One thing is certain: it will be different. Staff retention, after the higher cost of training, will be paramount. Mentors must be sensitive to this new emphasis and be geared to play a positive role in its progress.

New Industries

New industries, which may only now be dreamed of, will become reality. Think of the rapid growth of the information technology industry which, at times, seems to dominate the industrial world. Mentors are not expected to be inventors. But they must keep abreast of developments. Basic principles of mentoring may not change in the new scenario. However, the new art will be awareness of the implications and applications of new industries, familiarity with the new terminology and ability to appreciate how mentoring fundamentals are still relevant.

Review of Databases

Databases are the platforms for, or engines that drive, the marketing and administration function. Contact programmes are indispensable in modern business. They are becoming, at the same time, more sophisticated and more user friendly. It is essential that mentors are up to date in the possibilities, functionality and management of databases and the computer programmes that process them.

Review of Training

In **Chapter 8**, we dealt with the training of mentors with particular reference to the transformation from boss, manager or executive, to mentor and guide. Future mentor training, induction and orientation programmes will take cognisance of the requirement to promote heightened human relations skills in the more stressful work environment created by advanced technology.

CHANGES IN MENTORING

We have mentioned the advisability of changing mentors during an assignment when it appears that a change of skill or the needs of better compatibility become apparent. The increasing pace of business means that decisiveness is expected. This expectation applies to mentoring also. It is not acceptable to mull over indefinitely whether or not to recommend a change of mentor or the addition of a specialist mentor. The mentoree will expect the mentor to come to a conclusion speedily.

Multiple Mentors

More than likely, future mentorees will be seen to require more than one mentor. This will arise from the increasing use of technology in all aspects of business. This is not to say that they do not need several mentors today, but rather that the ever-more rapid development of technology will highlight the requirement. The lead mentor will co-ordinate the activities of the other mentors, probably specialists in specific areas of business.

Telephone and Mobile

Mentoring by telephone is not beneficial. So much of mentoring is based on face-to-face contact where body language is important. That is not to say that telephone contact should not be used. It is helpful on occasion as an aid to the main contact programme.

Internet Mentoring

The possibilities of Internet mentoring are bound to be considered. There is an absence of face-to-face meetings and personal contact that we have come to expect. It is not a substitute for face-to-face mentoring. It is a fact that mentor/mentoree communication by telephone, fax and e-mail already occurs during the currency of an assignment.

Video conferencing may be the answer, in part at least. Even with international mentoring (which is more likely to happen when video conferencing is more widespread), personal contact meetings are essential.

Review of Organisation and Systems

From the foregoing it is clear that, because of the swiftness of commercial transformation, the organisation of the programme directorate will need to be kept under constant review, even more than previously. The upgrading of technology used will be continuous, staff training intensive and communication systems more user-friendly.

Board Rotation

In every organisation, rejuvenation is key to growth and development. The process starts at the top and cascades down. Its application at board level, at times, may seem insensitive because those who have given valuable service are asked to stand aside. It is not related to age because experience is often what is sought. It is about a fresh approach. Replacements will be drawn from all age groups to blend innovation, enterprise and experience. Those who leave will bring rejuvenation to other enterprises.

Internet Reporting

It is now fairly usual for mentors to report to the programme administration on an interactive basis on a web site. This practice is likely to increase as WAP phones, or their third-generation replacements, become more popular, versatile and flexible. These phones will enable the mentor to report online real-time immediately after a meeting.

11

THE MENTOR
THROUGH THE AGES

In this chapter, we review the origins of the concept of mentor.

The purpose of examining references to mentors in litera-ture is not merely to record mentions of such a character, but to identify utterances by them that may be useful for the modern mentor.

There are innumerable references to mentors and the mentoring process in literature, too many to include here. We have selected a representative sample that we have enjoyed. Each mentor will have his own favourites.

HISTORICAL BACKGROUND

Homer

Mentor, as a personality, first appears in the Greek classic, *The Iliad*, which, together with *The Odyssey*, the Greeks attributed to a single poet whom they named Homer.

In *The Iliad*, Mentor is variously described by translators as a horse-owner and as a horse-dealer. No more information about him is given in *The Iliad*, although he appears several times in several guises in *The Odyssey*.

Written in the late eighth or early seventh century BC, Mentor's initial appearance in this epic is not particularly auspicious. Having first been described as an old friend of Odysseus, who had entrusted the care of his whole household to him, he is addressed by Leocritus as a crazy fool or a mischief-maker. It looks as if his first piece of guidance was not well received!

Odysseus also had instructed Mentor, before his departure to Troy, to defer to the aged Laertes, father of Odysseus. It seems, from this instruction, that even he, Mentor, had someone to look to for guidance. Here is established one of the fundamental characteristics of a mentor — at the same time, both guide and student.

In *The Odyssey*, Athena, daughter of Zeus, and goddess of female arts, intelligence and war, and patroness of Odysseus, frequently disguised herself as Mentor. She appeared before Odysseus to assist him at critical times in his journey home. In that form, on one occasion, she addresses Telemachus, son of Odysseus, referring to his father,

> *He finished what he cared to say,*
> *And what he took in hand he brought to pass.*

Good advice to mentor and mentoree alike.

Mentor is both male and female, mortal and immortal — an androgynous demigod, half here, half there, wisdom personified. In the Robert Fitzgerald version of *The Odyssey*, the last word of the epic is the name, Mentor.

The Concise Oxford Dictionary defines an odyssey as "a series of wanderings; a long adventurous journey", an apt description of the mentoring process, which is often described as a journey undertaken by the mentor and mentoree together.

Beowulf

The Anglo-Saxon poem *Beowulf*, written sometime between the seventh and the end of the tenth century AD, contains a reference to a mentor in the Seamus Heaney version. Hrothgar laments the death of Aeschere:

> *He was Yrmenlaf's elder brother*
> *and a soul-mate to me, a true mentor,*
> *my right-hand man when the ranks clashed*
> *and our boar-crests had to take a battering*
> *in the line of action. Aeschere was everything*
> *the world admires in a wise man and a friend.*

Dante Alighieri (1265–1321)

Dante's *Divine Comedy*, written some time between 1308 and 1321, has Virgil as Dante's mentor on his journey from Hell to Purgatory. Some passages contain established principles of mentoring. A few examples will suffice:

One reason why a person might seek a mentor:

> *Like one who loves the gains he has amassed,*
> *And meets the hour when he must lose his loot,*
> *Distracted in his mind and all aghast.*

The supportive role of the mentor is observed in the form of encouragement:

> *I think my guide approved of what he heard —*
> *I think so, since he patiently attended*
> *With a pleased smile to each outspoken word.*

How protective a mentor ought to be is dealt with unequivocally:

> *And while I stood intent to gaze, my guide,*
> *Suddenly crying to me, "Look out! Look out!",*
> *Caught me where I stood, and pulled me to his side.*

Virgil passes the mentor process to Beatrice, who guides Dante to Paradise. This transfer to another mentor is part of the mentor process on some occasions.

> *If scaling to those Heights is your desire,*
> *There shall arrive a worthier than I,*
> *When I depart, and she will lead you higher.*

The art of listening is noted by Virgil (the mentor) who is recorded as saying:

> *My master, hearing this, looked to the right,*
> *Then turning round and facing me, he said:*
> *"He listens well who notes well what he hears."*

Abbé Fénelon (1651–1715)

The modern adoption of the name for wise counsellor derives from the book *The Adventures of Telemachus, son of Ulysses*, by

Archbishop François de Salignac de la Mothe Fénelon, published in 1699.

Adopting the Latin form of the Greek names (thus Ulysses for Odysseus, Minerva for Athena, etc.), Fénelon takes the story of the Odyssey, adds some parts of Virgil's *Aeneid* and uses the tale as a vehicle for Mentor to talk about many topics.

Fénelon's book is a virtual manual for mentors. A few quotations give some idea of the mentoring wisdom in this book.

The role of a mentor providing a wider perspective is shown to be necessary:

> *Those who govern in detail are always determined by the present, never extending their views to a distant future. They are always caught up in the affair of the day; and as their minds are engrossed by that alone, it makes too great an impression, and weakens the faculty of reason. For there is no forming a sound judgement of affairs but by comparing them all together, and ranging them in a certain order, so as to have sequence and proportion.*

The mentor asks questions to ascertain the consequences of contemplated actions and to seek other options.

> *Always weigh beforehand the consequences of everything you undertake. Endeavour to foresee the greatest misfortunes that may happen. And know that true courage consists in viewing danger at a distance, and despising it, when it cannot be avoided. For he that avoids thinking of it before it is to be feared will not have courage to support the sight of it when present. Whereas he who foresees all that can happen, who prevents all that can be prevented, and calmly encounters what cannot be avoided, alone deserves the character of wise and magnanimous.*

A mentor seeks to assess the skill and potential of the mentoree.

> *But to be able to form a sound judgement of men, you must begin with knowing what they ought to be. You must know in what solid merit consists, so that you may*

> *be capable of distinguishing between those who are*
> *possessed of it, and those who do not have it.*

A mentor must disengage from the mentoree at the end of an assignment. Fénelon describes the end of the process as Mentor (Minerva) prepares to leave Telemachus:

> *I am now going to leave you, son of Ulysses; but my wis-*
> *dom shall never leave you, provided you always retain a*
> *due sense of your inability to do anything well without it.*
> *It is now time that you should try to walk alone. The rea-*
> *son for my parting with you in Egypt and at Salente was*
> *to accustom you by degrees to be without me, as chil-*
> *dren are weaned, when it is time to take them from the*
> *breast and give them more solid food.*

At the end of *Telemachus*, "Mentor undergoes a metamorphosis and is revealed as Minerva (goddess of wisdom) . . . the real hero (i.e. Mentor) has already been resolved into pure Wisdom . . . the goddess . . . ascended into the air, enveloped in a cloud of gold and azure, and disappeared." Surely a worthy end to a mentoring assignment!

Note that, a few decades later, in Jean Jacques Rousseau's *Émile,* the eponymous pupil is given a copy of Fénelon's *Telemachus* to read when he comes of age.

Anthony Trollope (1815–1882)

In *Barchester Towers*, a young woman's mentoring and warnings to her sister-in-law have proved to be absolutely correct, and the recalcitrant mentoree is none too pleased by this outcome.

> *Mary Bold had turned mentor. That she [Eleanor Bold]*
> *could have forgiven had the mentor turned out to be in*
> *the wrong; but Mentors in the right are not to be par-*
> *doned.*

Paulo Coelho (1947–)

In *The Pilgrimage*, the Brazilian writer tells of his pilgrimage from the French border to Santiago de Compostela in Spain. His mentor is Petrus, an Italian industrial designer, who helps him to overcome the difficulties that he encounters on the way.

Here again, the theme is of a journey to achieve a defined goal. An experienced guide is provided who had previously made the pilgrimage accompanied by a mentor.

There are many words of wisdom in this book, such as:

> *. . . when you are moving toward an objective, it is very important to pay attention to the road. It is the road that teaches us the best way to get there, and the road enriches us as we walk its length.*

The author experiences many telling events, relevant to the process of mentoring, one of which was the following:

> *On the way I realised what was happening: I was guiding my guide. Furthermore, I realised that during our entire journey Petrus had never tried to appear wiser, holier, or better than I. All he had done was to transmit to me his experience of the RAM practices. Apart from this, he tried to show that he was human like everyone else . . . That fact made me feel stronger. Petrus was just another pilgrim . . .*

Cox and Stevens

In their book, *Selling the Wheel*, published in 2000, the authors create an imaginary world in ancient times. The main characters in the story, Max and Minnie, start a business based on Max's invention — the wheel. The book concentrates on their efforts to market and sell the wheel.

When they experience difficulties they seek guidance from a mentor called "the Oracle". Max and Minnie make frequent incursions into the mountains to seek the mentor, who listens carefully to their explanation of the difficulties they are experiencing and asks questions that lead them to the solution.

Surely this book is a must for mentors!

Appendix

CODE OF CONDUCT

A mentor's position of trust in the business community is founded not only on skill and commercial experience but also on a high standard of personal and professional behaviour.

At all times, a mentor shall uphold the good standing and reputation of the Mentor Programme.

In support of this, a mentor shall:

General Principles

1. Accept only those assignments for which he considers himself suitably qualified.

2. Maintain confidentiality about the commercial and financial affairs of an assigned enterprise.

3. Withdraw from an assignment, where there exists a conflict of interest, or a possible conflict of interest, or any other matter that makes it inadvisable to continue the assignment.

4. Refuse to accept, without the written permission of the Programme Director, an invitation to join the Board of an assigned company, an appointment as consultant to the assigned company, or to invest in the assigned company. Such permission will not be refused unless, in the opinion of the Director, it would be at variance with the spirit of the Mentor Programme.

5. Maintain the highest ethical standards. Should the mentor become aware of unethical practices within the assigned

enterprise, which the proprietors are unable or unwilling to rectify, the mentor shall resign from the assignment.

6. Have due regard for, and uphold, the law.

7. Refuse to accept or give any gift, favour or hospitality intended as, or having the effect of, bribery and corruption.

Mentor

8. Practise his art with conscience, objectivity, independence and dignity.

9. Perform his mentor duties in a time-efficient fashion.

10. Not canvass for assignments.

11. Not delegate to another person all or any part of an assignment.

12. Keep up-to-date on current business practices relating to matters relevant to mentor assignments.

13. Not permit considerations of religion, nationality, race, party politics, social standing or membership of a minority to influence his behaviour or approach to an assignment.

14. Be aware of, and sensitive to, the cultural environment within which he is working.

Mentoree

15. Develop a relationship based on mutual confidence.

16. Give to the mentoree and the mentoree's staff the courtesy, consideration and respect that is their due.

17. Regard the interests of the mentoree as his first consideration.

18. Ensure that the mentoree understands the nature and purpose of the mentoring assignment.

19. Be reliable in carrying out commitments made to the assigned enterprise.

20. Inform the mentoree of his intention to terminate an assignment, and the reasons for doing so, if he decides it is advisable for whatever reason.

21. Ensure that all forms of communication with a mentoree are clear and that the mentoree fully understands them.

22. Ensure that the mentoree does not become emotionally dependent on him.

23. Not pursue a personal relationship of an emotional or sexual nature with a mentoree or a mentoree's employees.

24. Take care not to drift into the management sphere.

25. Not recommend or write a reference for a mentoree or the mentoree's products or services.

Third Parties

26. Conduct himself with courtesy and consideration towards every person with whom he comes in contact during the course of an assignment.

27. Not make comments to the media about the Mentor Programme without the express permission of the Programme Director.

28. Have regard to the impact on the community and the environment of the business activities of the assigned enterprise.

29. Not permit motives of personal profit to influence the independent exercise of professional judgement in the mentoring relationship.

30. Behave towards his colleagues as he would have them behave towards him.

Administration

31. Submit reports about an assignment in the format required and as often as requested by the Programme Director.

32. Report to the Programme Director any matter arising within an assignment that affects or might affect the Mentor Programme

33. Be familiar with the contents of the Mentor Manual.

34. Recommend to the Programme Director that another mentor be appointed to an assignment to provide an additional or alternative skill/experience that he deems would be useful to the mentoree. In such an event, the Programme Director will ensure that there is an efficient communications link between the two mentors. The Programme Director will make it clear to both mentors which mentor is responsible for the satisfactory completion of the assignment.

35. Inform the Programme Director whenever an assignment is beyond his capacity and suggest the appointment of another mentor who has the necessary ability.

36. Provide the replacement mentor with all assistance possible to assist in the achievement of a successful outcome to the assignment when the original mentor disengages from an assignment and another mentor is appointed.

BIBLIOGRAPHY

The following books are about in-company mentoring. Nevertheless, readers may find them of interest.

Bentley, T., *Motivating People*, McGraw-Hill, 1996.

Burley-Allen, Madelyn, *Listening*, James Wilson, 1995.

Carew, Jack, *The Mentor*, Plume, 1999.

Clutterbuck, D., *Everyone Needs a Mentor*, Institute of Personnel and Development, 1991.

Conway, Christopher, *Strategies for Mentoring*, John Wiley and Sons, 1998.

Daloz, Laurent A., *Mentor*, Jossey Bass, 1999.

Davidson, J.P., *Essential Management Checklists*, Kogan Page, 1987.

Deeprose, D., *The Team Coach*, American Management Association, 1995.

Hamilton, R., *Mentoring*, The Industrial Society, 1993.

Institute of Personnel and Development, *Counselling at Work*, 1997.

Kalinauckas, P. and King, H., *Coaching*, Institute of Personnel and Development, 1994.

Levinson, Daniel J., *The Seasons of a Man's Life*, Ballantine Books, 1978.

Mumford, A., *Management Development*, Institute of Personnel and Development, 1993.

Norton, B. and Tivey, J., *Mentoring*, Institute of Management, 1993.

Parsloe, E., *Coaching, Mentoring and Assessing*, Kogan Page, London, 1992.

Salacuse, J.W., *The Art of Advice*, Time Books, 1994.

Savidge, Jack, *New Resources: Mentors, Coaches, Gurus and Angels*, The Finnish Academies of Technology.

Shea, Gordon F., *Mentoring/Helping Employees Reach Their Full Potential*, Kogan Page, 1992.

Summerfield, J. and van Oudtshoorn, L., *Counselling in the Workplace*, Institute of Personnel and Development, 1995.

Vos, T., *Coaching*, McGraw Hill, 1997.

Videos
Burley-Allen, Madelyn, *Succeed by Listening*, James Wilson, 1995.

Cassettes/Tapes
Woodring, S.F., *Mentoring*, CareerTrack Publications, 1992.

INDEX

Starting Your Own Business: A Workbook

Second Irish edition
Ron Immink and Brian O'Kane
ISBN 1-86076-224-7, £14.95, paperback

Starting Your Own Business: A Workbook was originally commissioned in 1997 by the Department of Enterprise, Trade and Employment under Measure 4 of the Operational Programme for Small Business to meet a real need for practical, relevant information among would-be entrepreneurs. Now the book has been updated and expanded, to include new sections on e-business and working from home, reflecting the changing trends in Irish small business.

The guide takes a potential entrepreneur through the whole process of starting a business, from first thoughts about self-employment to the practicalities of start-up. It consists of three chapters, filled with checklists, flowcharts and questionnaires:

- **READY** provides essential background information, preparatory to making a commitment to a start-up. It includes both Self-assessment and Market research as key elements, as well as Training for Entrepreneurs and Start-up alternatives.

- **STEADY** goes through the steps necessary to develop a Business Plan, including Mission Statement, Strategy, Marketing, Staff, Finance, Taxation and Premises. Presenting the Business Plan and Financiers' views on Business Plans are also included.

- **GO** provides forms and documentation to help you put your business into action.

Templates and spreadsheets for key elements of the business plan can be downloaded from ***www.startingabusinessinireland.com***, which also includes updates and other information.

Forthcoming:

Starting Your Own Business (UK edition)

Terry Owens, Ron Immink and Brian O'Kane
ISBN 1-86076-226-3

A new edition of the Irish bestseller, *Starting Your Own Business: A Workbook*, will shortly be available in a UK edition, linked to a supporting website, ***www.startingabusinessinbritain.com***.

Successful Micro Entrepreneurship
Applying the Rules of Business

Ron Immink and Brian O'Kane
Start-up edition: ISBN 1-86076-231-X
Developing business edition: ISBN 1-86076-232-8

A decade's experience of sharing entrepreneurial know-how is encapsulated in these short guides, which explain the "rules of business" that apply to businesses of all sizes. They lead the potential entrepreneur through an intuitive process, at the end of which they have prepared a simple but effective business plan.

Also available:

Creating and Developing a Consultancy Practice by Martin Wilson, ISBN 1-86076-044-9

The Effective Consultant by Paul Mooney, ISBN 1-86076-121-6

The European Handbook of Management Consultancy,
ISBN 1-86076-010-4 (hardback); 1-86076-046-5

All of the books listed above can be ordered from Oak Tree Press, 19 Rutland Street, Cork, Ireland.
Telephone: (+353-21) 4313 855 Fax: (+353-21) 4313 496
E-mail: orders@oaktreepress.com
Web: www.oaktreepress.com

Oak Tree Press

**For more information on mentoring entrepreneurs,
visit <u>www.mentoringentrepreneurs.com</u>, a companion
website to this book.**